Mnemonics for Study

Also by Fiona McPherson

Effective Notetaking (Study Skills)
Planning to Remember: How to remember what you're
doing and what you plan to do
Perfect Memory Training

Mnemonics for Study

Strategies to help you memorize effectively

Fiona McPherson

Wayz Press
Wellington, New Zealand

Published by Wayz Press, an imprint of Capital Research Limited, 31 Gloucester Street, Wellington, New Zealand.

ISBN 978-0-9876522-0-1

To report errors, please email errata@wayz.co.nz

For additional resources and up-to-date information about any errors, go to the Mempowered website at www.mempowered.com

Contents

Introduction to mnemonics

WHAT ARE MNEMONICS AND WHAT ARE THEY GOOD FOR?

Any memory-improving strategy can be termed "mnemonic", but in its more specific meaning, mnemonic refers to "artificial" memory aids such as stories, rhymes, acronyms, and more complex strategies involving verbal mediators or visual imagery, such as the place or journey method, the pegword method, and the keyword method.

We will get to each of these in due course, but first we need to consider the benefits and limitations of such mnemonics, and in particular when you should use them in the course of study and when you should not.

The most important thing to understand is that mnemonics do *not* help you understand your material. They do not help with comprehension; they do not help you make meaningful connections.

The purpose of mnemonics is simply to help you remember something — not by understanding it, not by incorporating it into your developing "expert database", but simply in the manner of a parrot. They are used to enable you to regurgitate information.

That sounds terribly contemptuous, but if I considered there was no value in mnemonics I wouldn't be devoting this book to them. The ability to regurgitate information on demand is undeniably a useful one — indeed, in the context of examinations, often a vital one!

Even in the context of material you need to understand, there are often details that must simply be memorized — names of things, technical words, lists of principles, and so on. Moreover, mnemonics can help you remember tags or labels that allow you to access clusters of meaningful information — for example, headings of a speech or main points for exam essays. For both these reasons, mnemonics are a valuable assistance to building up expertise in a subject, as well as in helping you 'cram' for an exam.

However, despite a number of studies showing the effectiveness of mnemonic strategies, these remain the least frequently used formal memory aid used by students[1]. Perhaps the main reason for this is that their effectiveness is not intuitively obvious — truly, no one really believes that these 'tricks' can so remarkably improve memory until they try them for themselves.

But I can help you believe (and belief is vital if you're going to make the effort to use, and keep on using, any memory strategy) if I explain why they work. It's also important to understand the principles involved if you're going to fully the master these techniques — by which I mean, know when and when not to use them, and how to use them flexibly.

Do note that this is a very bare-bones account of the principles. For more details, I refer you to my book *The Memory Key*, available as a digital book from my website, or to the revised paperback edition, *Perfect Memory Training*.

WHY ARE MNEMONICS EFFECTIVE?

Let's think about the basic principles of how memory works.

The strength of memory codes, and thus the ease with which they can be found, is a function largely of repetition. (For those who haven't read *The Memory Key*, let me note that I habitually refer to information encoded in memory as memory codes to emphasize that memories are not faithful and complete recordings, but highly selected and edited.) Quite simply, the more often you experience something (a word, an event, a person, anything), the stronger and more easily recalled your memory for that thing will be.

This is why the most basic memory strategy — the simplest, and the first learned — is rote repetition.

Repetition is how we hold items in working memory, that is, "in mind". When we are told a phone number and have to remember it long enough to either dial it or write it down, most of us repeat it frantically. This is because we can only hold something in working memory by keeping it active, and this is the simplest way of doing so.

Spaced repetition — repetition at intervals of time — is how we cement most of our memory codes in our long-term memory store. If you make no deliberate attempt to learn a phone number, yet use it often, you will inevitably come to know it (although how many repetitions that will take depends on several factors, including individual variability).

But most of us come to realize that repetition is not, on its own, the most effective strategy for learning, and when we deliberately wish to learn something, we generally incorporate other, more elaborative, strategies.

Why do we do that? If memory codes are strengthened by repetition, why isn't it enough to simply repeat?

Well, it is. Repetition IS enough. But it's boring. That's point one.

Point two is that making memory codes more easily found (which is after all the point of the exercise) is not solely achieved by making the memory codes stronger. Also important is making lots of connections. Memory codes are held in a network. We find a particular one by following a trail of linked codes. Clearly, the more trails that lead to the code you're looking for, the more likely you are to find it.

Elaborative strategies — mnemonic strategies, organizational strategies — work on this aspect. They are designed to increase the number of links (connections) a memory code has, and therefore the number of different routes you can take to it.

Thus, when we note that a lamprey is an "eel-like aquatic vertebrate with sucker mouth", we will probably make links with eels, with fish, with the sea. If we recall that Henry I was said to have died from a surfeit of lampreys, we have made another link. Which in turn might bring in yet another link, that Ngaio Marsh once wrote a mystery entitled "A surfeit of lampreys". And if you've read the book, this will be a good link, being itself rich in links. (As the earlier link would be if you happen to be knowledgeable about Henry I).

4

On the other hand, in the absence of any knowledge about lampreys, you could have made a mnemonic link with the word "lamp", and imagined an eel-like fish with lamps in its eyes.

So, both types of elaborative strategy have the same goal — to increase the number of connections. But mnemonic links are weaker in the sense that they are arbitrary. Their value comes in those circumstances when either you lack the knowledge to make meaningful connections, or there is in fact no meaningful connection to be made.

Mnemonic strategies have therefore had particular success in the learning of other languages. However, if you *can* make a meaningful connection, that will be more effective.

For example, in Spanish the word *surgir* means to appear, arise. If you connect this to the word *surge*, from the Latin *surgere*, to rise, then you have a meaningful connection, and you won't, it is clear, have much trouble when you come across the word. However, if your English vocabulary does not include the word *surge*, you might make instead a mnemonic connection, such as *surgir* sounds like *sugar*, so you make a mental image involving rising sugar.

Now, consider each of these situations. Say you don't come across the word again for a month. When you do, which of these connections is more likely to bring forth the correct meaning?

But of course, it is not always possible to make meaningful connections (either because there are no meaningful connections to be made, or because you don't have the necessary information to make meaningful connections), and this is where mnemonics are so useful.

Additionally, sequence is often not obviously meaningful (although it may become so when you have a deeper understanding of the subject), and mnemonics are particularly good for ordered information.

The thing to remember, however, is that even with mnemonic strategies, you haven't overcome the need for repetition. The basic principle must always be remembered: Memory codes are made stronger by repetition. Links are made stronger by repetition. If you don't practice the mnemonic, it won't be remembered.

The same is true for any connection, but meaningful connections are inherently stronger, so they don't need as many repetitions.

Points to Remember

Memory codes are made stronger by repetition.

Memory codes are made easier to find by increasing the number of links they have to other memory codes.

Elaborative strategies make links with existing codes.

Meaningful links between memory codes are stronger.

Mnemonic strategies make links that are not meaningful.

Mnemonic strategies are most useful:

— where there are no meaningful connections to be made, or you lack the knowledge to make meaningful connections

— where you need to remember items in sequence.

ABOUT IMAGERY

The more complex mnemonic strategies are usually based on visual images. This causes people who feel that their ability to 'see' mental images is poor to think that mnemonics are of no use to them. That would be overly hasty. Although imagery is certainly an effective tool, there is nothing particularly special about it. The big advantage of imagery is that it provides an easy way of connecting information that is not otherwise readily connected. However, providing verbal links can be equally effective.

Individual differences

Moreover, although there is undoubtedly considerable variation between people in terms of their abilities to visualize images, only a very small percentage of people *don't* visualize. A similarly small percentage makes extremely vivid images. Somewhere in between are the rest of us.

My own feeling is that many people don't realize the extent to which they form visual images. You don't need clear television-quality mental images to visualize usefully! When you're reading a novel, for example, you may well have no conscious awareness of the pictures being created in your mind, but if you see a movie adaptation of the book you'll immediately notice all the visual images that are 'wrong' (such as what the hero looks like).

If you're uncertain about your visualization abilities, you might find these signs interesting:

High visualizers are more easily tricked into thinking imagined experiences have really happened — they create false memories more easily.

There's also some evidence[2] that high visualizers are better at fighting the Stroop effect. The Stroop effect concerns color-name interference: when you see the name of a color written in the same color, that's easier to process than when the color doesn't match the name (for example, 'red' written in blue ink). Comparison of the different reaction times (how long it takes you to process **RED** written in red ink compared to **RED** written in blue ink) has been used to test attention, executive function, and processing speed, and less directly the presence of various disorders.

More recently a study that looked at differences in brain activity as people imagined a visual scene, found that not only were there noticeable differences between good and poor visualizers (good visualizers had more activity in their visual cortex), but that this correlated with performance on the Stroop test. Those showing greater activity in their visual cortex (good visualizers) were *slower* at naming colors when the names *matched* the color they were written in (this is of course the opposite of what is usually found). This is a very small study (8 people) and we can't draw too firm a conclusion, but it is interesting. There are places on the web where you can get a feel for your performance on this task (for example, www.snre.umich.edu/eplab/demos/st0/stroopdesc.html).

But the most important thing to note is that visualization is a skill that is strengthened with practice. If you persevere with trying to make good visual images, you will get better at it.

Using imagery

For myself, I am very verbal (not surprising in a writer!), but that doesn't mean images, albeit not particularly vivid ones, aren't being formed in my mind. What I find works best for me, and probably what will work best for most of you, if you're not at the extreme ends of visualization ability, is the use of both words and images. That is, when you're using a verbal mnemonic, aim for words that are easy to visualize; when you're using a visual mnemonic, make sure the pictures have associated word labels, and keep them in mind while you're imagining the picture.

Most mnemonic strategies, despite being usually described as 'visual' or 'verbal', do in fact combine both aspects, and you may emphasize the visual *or* the verbal aspect as suits you.

It is usually emphasized that bizarre images are remembered much better, but there is no clear evidence for this. Indeed in many studies ordinary images are remembered slightly better. One of the problems is that people usually find it harder to create bizarre images. Unless you have a natural talent for thinking up bizarre images, it is probably not worth bothering about.

Whether bizarre or not, images generally take longer to construct than verbal phrases. If you want to construct them 'on the fly', as you hear information in conversation or in a presentation like a lecture, then you need to have practiced the skill a great deal.

The critical point to remember is that images, and words, work well as mnemonics only to the extent that they are bound together. Thus, an image needs to be *interactive* — tying the bits of information tightly together.

Don't worry if you're not sure exactly what this means! It will become clear as we discuss the various mnemonic techniques. For now, I just ask you to bear it in mind.

Points to Remember

Images are effective to the extent that they link information.

Images are not inherently superior to words.

Bizarre images are not necessarily better recalled than common ones.

Effective images involve the elements interacting with each other.

Part I
Simple Verbal Mnemonics

In this section, we're going to explore some simple verbal mnemonics that you will already be familiar with — acronyms, acrostics, rhymes, and songs.

First-letter mnemonics

TWO TYPES OF FIRST-LETTER MNEMONICS

First-letter mnemonics are, as their name suggests, memory strategies that use the initial letters of words as aids to remembering. This can be an effective technique because initial letters are helpful retrieval cues, as anyone who has endeavored to remember something by mentally running through the letters of the alphabet can attest to.

There are two types of first-letter mnemonic:

- **acronyms:** initial letters form a meaningful word;

- **acrostics:** initial letters are used as the initial letters of other words to make a meaningful phrase

ROY G. BIV is an acronym (for the colors of the rainbow), and **R**ichard **O**f **Y**ork **G**ives **B**attle **I**n **V**ain is an acrostic for the same information.

Similarly, the acronym **FACE** is used to remember the notes in the spaces of the treble staff, and the acrostic **E**very **G**ood **B**oy **D**eserves **F**ruit for the notes on the lines of the treble staff.

Here are some more well-known ones. Acronyms first:

HOMES — the Great Lakes: **H**uron; **O**ntario; **M**ichigan; **E**rie; **S**uperior.

MRS GREN — the characteristics of living things: **M**ovement; **R**espiration; **S**ensitivity; **G**rowth; **R**eproduction; **E**xcretion; **N**utrition.

BEDMAS — the order of mathematical operations: **B**rackets; **E**xponent; **D**ivision; **M**ultiplication; **A**ddition; **S**ubtraction.

SOH-CAH-TOA — **S**in is **O**pposite **H**ypotenuse; **C**os is **A**djacent to the **H**ypotenuse; **T**an is **O**pposite the Adjacent.

And some acrostics:

My **V**ery **E**ager **M**other **J**ust **S**erved **U**s **N**ine **P**izzas — the order of the planets: **M**ercury; **V**enus; **E**arth; **M**ars; **J**upiter; **S**aturn; **U**ranus; **N**eptune; **P**luto.

Father **C**harles **G**oes **D**own **A**nd **E**nds **B**attle — the order of sharps in music.

King **P**hillip **C**ame **O**ver **F**rom **G**reat **S**pain — the order of categories in the taxonomy of living things (**K**ingdom **P**hylum **C**lass **O**rder **F**amily **G**enus **S**pecies).

It's likely that you'll know very different acrostics for these same items. That's one difference between acronyms and acrostics — the same acronyms are likely to be known to everyone, but acrostics are much more varied. The reason's not hard to seek — clearly there are infinite possibilities for acrostics, but very very limited possibilities for acronyms.

This means, of course, that opportunities to use acronyms are also very limited. It is only rarely that the initial letters of a group of items you wish to learn will form a word or series of words or at least a pseudo-word (a series of letters that do not form a word but are pronounceable as one — like BEDMAS).

Nothing is going to make MVEMJSUNP (the order of planets) memorable in itself, even if you break it up into vaguely intelligible bits, like this: M.V. Em J. Sun P. (although that does help — say it and you'll see why).

Acrostics, on the other hand, are easy to create, and any string of items can be expressed in that form. For example:

My **V**ery **E**arnest **M**other **J**umped **S**even **U**mbrellas **N**ear **P**aris

Men **V**iew **E**nemies **M**ildly **J**uiced **S**ince **U**nited **N**ations **P**arty

Michael **V**oted **E**very **M**ay **J**udiciously **S**ince **U**nion **N**ewsletters **P**lunged

I created those as I typed; it's not difficult. But of course the aim is not simply to devise acrostics, it's to create *good* acrostics. That is, memorable ones. That's not quite as easy.

HOW TO CREATE EFFECTIVE ACROSTICS

Let's start with one of the best-known mnemonics in

geography, in the United States at least: HOMES — an acronym for the Great Lakes. Less well-known are sentence mnemonics to help you remember the geographical order of the lakes (from west to east or east to west), or their relative size. There are a few around. Here's some I made up:

Simon **M**akes **H**erons **E**at **O**lives (the Great Lakes from west to east)

Oliver **E**ats **H**errings **M**arinated **S**lowly (from east to west)

Simon **H**as **M**any **E**legant **O**wls (in order of size)

Now, these are all useful mnemonics, but they are only useful in very particular circumstances, glaringly obvious to non-North Americans at least. Namely, you need to already know the names of the Great Lakes.

All the lakes have fairly obvious cues: Superior is a familiar word; Erie is very close to the word eerie; Huron is very close to heron; both Ontario and Michigan are names for the province/ state they're in. So if you aren't that familiar with the names of the lakes, rather than HOMES, you would be better with an acrostic like this one:

A heron is superior in Ontario but eerie in Michigan.

In fact, because HOMES is such a good acronym, being a short, very familiar word, the best mnemonic would be:

A heron is superior in Ontario but eerie in Michigan HOMES.

This sentence makes sense, and ties the two mnemonics together. This is good because both have value, and have slightly different functions. HOMES is much easier to remember and provides valuable first-letter retrieval cues; the acrostic provides more detailed cues for the items.

Neither the acrostic nor the acronym provides any order information however. But if you look back at my suggested acrostics for order, you'll see there are two obvious problems with these: they provide no information to help you with remembering the items themselves other than the first-letter retrieval cues, and they provide no clues to tell you what particular order is being specified.

Here are some examples that might be better for size order:

Simon **H**as **M**any **E**normous **O**wls

Superior **H**erons **M**ight **E**at **O**wls

Superior **H**erons **M**ight **E**at **O**reos

Sizing **H**erons **M**ight **E**fface **O**wls

These words are better reminders of the items, for the most part. "Owls" is not a good cue for Ontario, but unfortunately (though not uncommonly), there are few words reminiscent of Ontario! "Oreos" is probably a better one, but only for those who are familiar with Oreos (personally, not being an American, I know of them only by repute — which isn't really enough to make them a good cue for me).

"Superior" might be a good enough cue for you to put the acrostic in its proper context, because superior does vaguely have connotations of size. But it may not — hence the suggested use of "Sizing" instead of "Superior". On the other hand, "Sizing" is not a particularly good cue for "Superior".

So which of these words would be more effective for you depends on whether it's more important for you to have a clue to the name or the function of the acrostic.

The clue to context doesn't have to be in the first word (in the first example, the fourth word, "Enormous", is the clue), but I suspect it's a good idea, where possible.

Here are some examples for direction order that incorporate hints that direction provides the order:

From east to west:

Oriental **E**nemies **H**ave **M**arine **S**nails

Oriental **E**ast **H**eads **M**ore **S**unset

The first of these makes a little more sense, but only the first word provides a clue to the context (east to west). The second is full of clues that this is about direction and the direction is east to west, but doesn't really make sense as a sentence. Neither provides any clues to the items themselves; they are there only to provide first-letter retrieval cues.

Maybe we'll have more luck with the opposite direction (you only need to know either west or east, *or* east to west, after all!).

From west to east:

Sunset **M**oves **H**eavily **E**ast **O**rientally

Sunset **M**oves **H**eavily **E**ast [to the] **O**rient

Simon **M**ay **H**ead **E**ast **O**ccasionally

These examples confirm what was suggested in the earlier examples — you can't provide both direction clues and content clues; the words can't bear the double burden. You have to choose which is more important to you.

Or, of course, learn two separate mnemonics (or indeed, three, if size is also important to you). There's no particular problem with that, as long as the mnemonics provide the needed cues as to context.

The first two of this last group of acrostics (**S**unset **M**oves **H**eavily **E**ast **O**rientally; **S**unset **M**oves **H**eavily **E**ast [to the] **O**rient) also provide examples of two permissible actions: making up words ("orientally"), and putting in small words that don't count (i.e., they're not to be considered when pulling out the first-letter cues; they're only there to help the acrostic make sense).

I say these actions are permissible; I don't say they're desirable. Both should only be resorted to when better alternatives fail, for invented words are less memorable, and redundant words are potentially confusing.

The last example I give (**S**imon **M**ay **H**ead **E**ast **O**ccasionally) makes more sense and doesn't have these drawbacks; it doesn't, however, have the context clue in the first word. On the other hand, I think the sentence as a whole provides a strong enough context clue that this doesn't matter (the point being, that a coherent sentence will be treated more readily as a whole, rather than processed word by word).

This analysis has, I hoped, suggested a number of rules for creating effective first-letter mnemonics, but before we summarize these, we need to consider some problems with this type of mnemonic.

PROBLEMS WITH FIRST-LETTER MNEMONICS

Medical students are probably the group who use first-letter mnemonics most. Here's a medical example that demonstrates a common problem with first-letter mnemonics:

On **O**ld **O**lympia's **T**owering **T**op **A** **F**inn **A**nd **G**erman **V**ault **A**nd **H**op

This is a mnemonic for remembering the cranial nerves: olfactory, optic, oculomotor, trochlear, trigeminal, abducens, facial, auditory, glossopharyngeal, vagus, accessory, and hypoglossal. Of course, reiterating my earlier point, the mnemonic wouldn't help most of us remember this information, because we don't know these names. But there's another problem with this acrostic: three Os, two Ts and three As.

This is a particular problem when the purpose of the acrostic is to remind you of the precise order of items, for obvious reasons. In such a case, you need to use words that distinguish between similar items.

Thus, a better acrostic for our medical students might be:

Oliver **Op**erates **Oc**casional **Tro**pical **Tri**cks **Ab**surdly **F**or **Au**stralian **G**ymnasts **V**aulting **Ac**tual **H**elicopters

Except that the traditional acrostic does have two big advantages that make it a much more memorable sentence: rhythm and rhyme. Say them both aloud, and you'll see what I mean.

Let's try for an acrostic that contains the vital information *and* is memorable.

Oliver **Op**ens **Oc**eans; **Tro**pical **Tri**ps **Ab**et; **F**abulous **Au**thors **G**ushing; **V**iolent **Ac**ts **H**inted

Okay, this isn't very good either, and it took a little while to come up with. I've tried to distinguish the same-initial terms by including the second letter. The problem is, this additional constraint makes a big difference in limiting the possibilities.

Also, of course, creating an acrostic with rhyme and rhythm requires a great deal more work than simply creating a meaningful sentence. Rhyme and rhythm do, however, render the acrostic considerably more memorable.

In fact, were I trying to memorize the 12 cranial nerves, I wouldn't use a first-letter mnemonic. Let us consider what you need to learn:

- The names of each nerve

- The function of each nerve

- The order of each nerve

The cranial nerves are not simply in a particular order; they are numbered. This immediately suggests the appropriate mnemonic: the pegword mnemonic. And the need to remember some rather strange names, and associate this information with function, suggests another useful mnemonic: the keyword mnemonic. I return to this example in the discussions of those mnemonics.

Before getting to the guidelines for creating good first-letter mnemonics, there's one more aspect we need to consider — *when* first-letter mnemonics are useful.

WHEN FIRST-LETTER MNEMONICS ARE A GOOD STRATEGY

As I implied earlier, first-letter mnemonics are effective because initial letters make good retrieval cues. But there's another critical point that's less obvious.

Several studies have found that first-letter mnemonics are of no particular benefit in helping remember, but in all these cases, students were asked to learn unrelated words[1]. However, one study found there *was* a benefit when the *order* of items became important[2], and further investigation confirmed that while the mnemonic isn't useful for learning new sets of unrelated items, it does help when the items themselves don't have to be learned, but the order of them does[3].

The same study also confirmed that, by an overwhelming margin, the chief type of error made by those using a first-letter mnemonic is that of reversal — that is, confusing an item with another item with the same initial.

So, it seems that first-letter mnemonics are of no particular benefit when order isn't important, although if the items in a list lend themselves to a memorable acronym (such as HOMES), then you should certainly take advantage of that fact. Such opportunities will, however, be rare.

Acrostics are much more widely applicable, but generally less memorable than acronyms.

So when are first-letter mnemonics a good strategy to use?

The best time is when you have a relatively short list of

items, with very familiar items that all begin with different initials. Items should be related — related items provide a much more limited set of possibilities for your initials, and are thus better retrieval cues.

The results of one study have also suggested that first-letter mnemonics may be more effective for females than males, for whom strategies involving visualization may be superior[4]. I imagine this reflects a broader preference of visual over verbal strategies, rather than a particular indictment of first-letter mnemonics however.

Because of their power as retrieval cues, first-letter mnemonics are also particularly recommended for students who suffer from exam anxiety, with consequent memory blocks (having your mind go blank when you look at the exam questions).

Teachers and writers might also like to note a study that found that giving the initial letters of the main points of a concrete (but not an abstract) passage, either before or after the students read the passage, helped them retrieve the main points. Like other strategies that aid memory for particular items, it was however at the expense of remembering other details[5].

First-letter mnemonics are

- a cueing strategy, not a learning strategy

- useful when remembering the order is critical

- useful when you want to prevent a memory block.

Principles for creating effective acrostics

Unfamiliar items need more cues. If the items are well-known, and the acrostic is only needed as a reminder or to provide order information, choice of words is only constrained by initial letter. However, if the items are not well-known, the words must also provide cues to the items.

Choose familiar words. Where possible, the words chosen should be familiar words (which are more easily recalled).

Make it meaningful. As much as possible, the acrostic itself should make coherent sense (a meaningful sentence is remembered more easily).

Cue the order. If the acrostic is providing a particular type of order, where more than one type is possible, than it needs to also contain cues to what kind of order is involved.

Keep it simple (don't force your mnemonic to carry too much information). If the acrostic is required to bear information about order, kind of order, and item content, it is usually better to create more than one mnemonic.

Rhythm & rhyme

SOME FAMILIAR MNEMONIC JINGLES

Thirty days hath September,

April, June and November.

All the rest have 31,

Excepting February alone,

And that has 28 days clear,

And 29 in each leap year.

Many of you will know this jingle, or a variant. I learned this in childhood, and to this day, when I want to know the number of days in the month (and it's something that comes up surprisingly often), I run through the first two lines.

The first two lines are all that are needed in most circumstances, once you're familiar with the verse. I don't need the mnemonic to tell me how many days February has, but I do still like to make sure I have the vexed 30-31 question right!

Rhythm and rhyme are powerful aids to memory, but the

reason this jingle comes so easily to mind is not because of those two factors alone — it's because of the frequent repetition I've given it. This is something that needs to be borne in mind with all mnemonics — mnemonics make remembering easier, but they don't obliterate the need for repetition. They simply reduce it. Indeed, you could say one measure of how effective a mnemonic is, is the degree to which it reduces the need for repetition.

Here's another little jingle that will be familiar to many:

> In fourteen hundred and ninety-two,
>
> Columbus sailed the ocean blue

Isn't it remarkable how much more memorable the addition of a simple rhyme and a meter makes this? Compare it to: In fourteen ninety-two, Columbus crossed the Atlantic.

Here's one that might be more familiar to British and Commonwealth citizens, commemorating Guy Fawkes Day:

> Remember remember,
>
> The 5th of November,
>
> Gunpowder, treason and plot.

It's all about rhythm and rhyme.

Rhyme is an effective cue to remembering for similar reasons as first-letter mnemonics: because of the way words are filed in memory, and because it provides constraints on the possibilities. Think of songs and poems that you can easily finish the line for, simply because the word seems obvious — because of the constraints of context and rhyme.

That tells us something. It tells us that an important variable in deciding whether a rhyme is effective is the extent to which it is **predictable**. Predictable rhymes, although it may seem counter-intuitive, are generally more effective — hence the banality of most popular and durable mnemonic verses.

Rhythm is a little more complex. Rhythm takes us to music, and perhaps we should start by considering why music helps us to remember. Or *how* it helps us remember.

SINGING TO REMEMBER

Research has convincingly demonstrated that words are more easily recalled when they are learned as a song rather than speech, but *only* in particular conditions. The important thing is the melody.

The reason melody can be useful is, again, because it provides cues to recall — by virtue of the constraints they place on the possibilities, particularly in terms of line and syllable length. So if melody is to be useful, it is crucial that it be simple and predictable (like rhythm).

Simplicity is not a rigid measure of course. What is simple to one person, particularly a musically trained one, may not be simple to another. Simplicity also varies with familiarity — the more often we hear a melody, the simpler it will become.

An important aspect of simplicity is that the text and the music should be closely integrated — specifically, the number of notes in the melody should match the number of syllables in the lyrics.

Simplicity and familiarity are why, if you want to improve memorability by attaching the material you want to remember to a tune, you are advised to choose a familiar 'nursery' song.

Simplicity also impacts on predictability. Predictability is important for the obvious reason that melody helps us remember text to the extent that it provides cues, but also because we remember expected information better[1].

As far as the lyrics themselves are concerned, context is also an important factor. We can predict the words in a song or poem not simply because of the constraints of rhyme and rhythm, but also because the context sets its own restraints. We know that in a love song, *heart* might rhyme with *part* (e.g., *we'll never part*), but is never going to rhyme with *fart* (unless it's a parody!).

This tells us that related text — text that is coherent and meaningful, that belongs together — is going to be much more effective than unrelated text (such as a list of words).

That doesn't mean that unrelated text won't be helped by attaching it to a tune. One study[2] found that, although hearing a list of words sung didn't help people learn the words any better than hearing them spoken, nevertheless, those who heard them sung took less time to relearn the list a week later. However, there are more effective ways of remembering unrelated items.

There are other reasons why music helps of course — reasons that have to do with motivation and emotion. Music engages us, and singing is fun. We're more likely to repeat a song much more often than a spoken passage. This simple fact — that the number of repetitions is high — accounts for a great deal of our memory for songs.

Attaching words to a melody shouldn't be taken as a magic bullet for remembering. But the fact that making something into a song does make it considerably more pleasurable shouldn't be ignored either.

Rules for mnemonic songs

Simple, well-known tune

Words that match the melody, note by note

Words framed in predictable, meaningful sentences and phrases

Lines that follow a predictable pattern and rhyme where possible

There are a number of songs that have been written to help with learning science — for example, Flanders & Swann's song describing the First and Second Laws of Thermodynamics, Tom Lehrer's song of the Periodic Table, as well as many more modern songs (did you know there was a Science Songwriters' Association?!) — as well as other subjects (such as Shakespearean prose). I have put links to a number of these on my website at www.mempowered/books/mnemonics-study/resources. You might find it useful to consider such songs in terms of these rules.

A practical example of a teaching song points to some other interesting issues. A study[3] was done involving a multimedia instructional module, using a computer animated sequence in conjunction with a song about the inner workings of a cell. The program was presented to 5th and 6th grade students by two different teachers. One of these teachers was happy to sing along; the other refused. There was a clear difference in the effectiveness of this program, depending on whether the teacher modeled the singing behavior or not.

There was also a clear gender difference, with girls being much happier with, and benefiting more from, the use of song. Partly this may be due to gender differences in music processing, but I suspect the main reason for this difference is cultural — the boys thought singing was "uncool" (a belief not helped, of course, by the male teacher refusing to sing himself).

SPOKEN RHYTHM

Let's return to rhythm on its own — spoken rhythm.

As with melody, research has had inconsistent results in determining its usefulness as a memory aid, and the reasons are probably the same.

It seems likely that rhythm is helpful to the extent that it:

- creates expectancies,

- sets constraints, and

- makes repetition more pleasurable.

It may also be that spoken rhythm is more likely to be effective as a mnemonic aid when it has a strong musical beat.

This would suggest that you will probably enhance memorability if you provide a back beat, most easily by clapping along with your words — but bear in mind that while synchronized physical movement can aid memory, it must be simple enough not to distract from the material you want learned.

It may also be that some rhythms are more effective aids than others. This is suggested by a study[4] that found that reciting the Iliad got the heart beating in time with the breath, which may improve gas exchange in the lungs as well as the body's sensitivity and responsiveness to blood pressure changes (blood flow, through its effect on oxygen flow, is critical for brain functioning). The researchers thought that it might be the hexametric pace of the Homeric verse that is critical for achieving this effect. They also suggested that such recitation produces "a feel-good effect".

Another study[5] found that vocalizing the Ave Maria in Latin or a yoga mantra slowed breathing and altered blood flow in the brain.

Dactylic hexameter (dum-diddy, dum-diddy, dum-diddy, dum-diddy, dum-diddy, dum-dum), which is the rhythm of classical epics, is unfortunately not one of the more common rhythms in English verse, but its musical counterpart — 6/8 time — is quite common.

However, it should be borne in mind that the most successful (widely used; long-lasting) mnemonic verses are all very short ones. Even the "30 days hath November" verse is one that, as I said, I only tend to use the first two lines of, and I confess I had to check my memory of the final three lines on the Web. The familiar aid to English spelling:

I before e, except after c

is one that rolls off my tongue with ease, but I didn't know (or had long forgotten) the rest:

I before E, except after C
And when saying "A" as in Neighbor or Weigh
And weird is weird.

(I also came across this variant, which demonstrates how accurate this "rule" is! — but still a useful rule-of-thumb:

I before E, except after C,

with the exceptions of Neither Financier Conceived Either Species of Weird Leisure.)

My point is that, although rhyme and rhythm are useful aids to memory, they are best restricted to very brief jingles. Although long poems have been constructed as mnemonic aids, you do need to put a lot of effort into memorizing them, and there are better strategies for mastering such long lists of facts (which we will get to).

Best Practices for Spoken Rhythm

Short jingles

Strong beat

Simple and predictable

Enjoyable

Part II
Keyword Strategies

The idea of a "keyword" is central to all the more complex mnemonic strategies. At its simplest, the idea reflects the fact that we remember new information by attaching it to information we already know well. This is why experts find it so much easier to learn new information (in their area of expertise) than novices — because they have a mass of related information that is already interwoven with many connections, and to which the new information can readily be connected.

However, not all information can be *meaningfully* connected to your existing information, and this is where the keyword comes in. The keyword is an intermediary that provides artificial meaning.

For example, to remember the name of the famous psychologist Alfred Binet, you could tie the name Binet to *bonnet* (the keyword) and imagine Binet in a bonnet. To remember that *aronga* means *direction* in Māori, you could give the unfamiliar word *aronga* the familiar word *wrong* as a keyword, and tie that to the meaning with the phrase *wrong direction*.

The use of keywords puts these strategies firmly into the category of **transformational elaborative strategies**. Elaboration — adding to and extending the information to be remembered — is one of the fundamental memory strategies, common to both transformational and non-transformational strategies. The term transformational, however, points to (and encapsulates the essence of) mnemonic strategies. This is what mnemonics are all about: transforming information into a form that makes it more memorable.

What you have to bear in mind, however, is that this transformation doesn't in any way add meaning. It will not help you understand the material. Its sole purpose is to add a memorable (but meaningless) connection.

For that reason transformational strategies should only be used when there aren't any meaningful connections (of sufficient memory power) that can be used. That still covers a lot of material!

The keyword method

The keyword mnemonic is the most studied mnemonic technique, and contains within it the most potential for flexible use in a wide range of learning situations.

The essence of this technique lies in the choosing of an intermediary word that binds what you need to remember to something you already know well.

For example, to remember that the Spanish word *carta* means letter (the sort you post), you select an English word that sounds as close to *carta* as you can get, and you make a mental picture that links that word to the English meaning — thus, a letter in a cart.

Or perhaps, to extend the technique a little further, you want to remember that Canberra is the capital of Australia. *Beer can* is an obvious phrase for Canberra (particularly in light of the Australians' notorious enjoyment of beer!), and you could connect it to Australia by substituting a familiar icon such as a kangaroo or a koala bear. Thus, your image for remembering this fact could be a kangaroo swigging back a can of beer.

We'll discuss the extension of this technique to fact learning in the next chapter. Let's first come to grips with the 'pure' technique, designed for learning new words — most especially for learning a new language, but equally applicable to learning new vocabulary (and every discipline has its own vocabulary).

SOME EXAMPLES TO PRACTISE

One of the early studies into the effectiveness of the keyword mnemonic for learning another language used transliterated Russian words. Russian is a good choice because it is much less likely to be familiar to English-speakers. Before looking further, try and come up with similar-sounding English words.

gorá	
durák	
ósen	
chelovék	
krovát	
dvor	
kusók	
rot	
naród	
úzhin	

I cruelly asked you to think of similar-sounding words before giving any details about the choosing of keywords, but I wanted you to have the experience of thinking of acoustically similar words before limiting you with that knowledge. Here are the ones the researchers (Atkinson & Raugh 1975) used:

gorá	garage
durák	two rocks
ósen	ocean
chelovék	chilly back
krovát	cravat
dvor	divorce
kusók	blue sock
rot	rut
naród	narrow road
úzhin	engine

Note that the important thing is *acoustic* similarity (Atkinson called it the acoustic link). It's all about *sounding* alike, not what the actual letters are.

Nor is it necessary to try and echo all of the word, although these words do. Obviously it is better if it does, but that is not always going to be possible. It is acceptable practice in those cases to echo only part of the word. For example, for *górod* (city), Atkinson & Raugh chose *go* as the keyword.

The next step is to create an imagery link with the meaning of the Russian word. Where it is difficult to create an image, you can make up a sentence or phrase that links the two. For example, the meaning of gorá is mountain, and this is easily linked in an image to our keyword "garage". However, although the meaning of the word chelovék is person, and this fits in perfectly with the keyword "chilly back", this is probably a clearer association in a phrase than in an image alone.

Here, in the third column, are the meanings of the words:

gorá	garage	**mountain**
durák	two rocks	**fool**
ósen	ocean	**autumn / fall**
chelovék	chilly back	**person**
krovát	cravat	**bed**
dvor	divorce	**yard, court**
kusók	blue sock	**piece**
rot	rut	**mouth**
naród	narrow road	**people**
úzhin	engine	**supper**

As a general rule, it is the thinking of the keyword that people find hard, not the creation of an image joining the two. But I'll offer some suggestions so you get the idea:

A garage perched on the summit of a mountain.

A jester trapped between two rocks.

A torrent of autumn leaves falling on the wide ocean.

A person shivering as a snowball splashes over his bare back.

A cravat laid out ready for wear on a bed.

In a yard, a judge decrees, and a man and woman separate.

Someone is cutting a large blue sock into pieces.

Deep ruts in a once-muddy road; one curves itself into a smile and then speaks, like a mouth.

A mass of people walking along a road that narrows, squeezing them tightly together.

Supper laid out on an exposed car engine.

If you have diligently tried to form these, or your own, images, you will have noticed that it is not entirely fair to call this an imagery link, or to make a distinction between an image and a sentence. In truth, both words and pictures are important. You need to make sure the crucial words — the keyword and the meaning — are attached to the images.

When you picture the people walking along a road that narrows, you need to be thinking *narrow road*, *people*;

when you see the snowball splashing on the person's bare back, you need to be thinking *chilly back, person.* It is after all the words that are critical — the images are there only to trigger the words.

So, you create a picture, and you think clearly about the words attached to the elements in the picture, and every time you recall the picture, you make sure you recall the words attached to the elements.

Another thing I hope you noticed when creating these images, is that the pictures I described were very bare-bones. When you turned my sentence into an image, there will have been details I didn't mention, details that are individual to you, to the way you think and the experiences you have had. That's good. While you shouldn't get bogged down in crafting very detailed images — indeed, you want to keep the images as simple as possible, so that the crucial elements are not hidden — you do want some details that make the images more memorable for you. How well these images work does depend on you putting in the effort to making them as clear and vivid as you can.

That does *not* mean that you have to be a brilliant visualizer to use this technique effectively!

As we have seen, the technique involves both words and images, which means that those who are highly visual can put more weight on images and those who are more verbal can put more weight on the words. But even those who do not think of themselves as particularly visual do benefit from images, so do make the effort (I assure you that you will get better with practice).

Let's try another example.

Here are some Spanish words for the classroom. Before looking at my suggestions (put a piece of paper over the text below), try and come up with English words that sound similar:

el lápiz		pencil
la papelera		wastepaper bin
las tijeras		scissors
la regla		ruler
las cuentas		sums
el pupitre		desk
el techo		ceiling
la pared		wall
el suelo		floor
el pincel		paintbrush

Here are some possibilities: lapel for el lápiz; puppet for la papelera; tiger for las tijeras; regatta for la regla; queen for las cuentas; pupil for el pupitre; teacher for el techo; parcel for la pared; swelling for el suelo; pencil for el pincel.

The next step is to make an image joining the keyword and the meaning. Here are mine:

A big pencil sticking out of a jacket's lapel (where a flower or pin might be).

A puppet hanging over the edge of the wastepaper bin.

Baby tigers running around the classroom waving scissors.

A fleet of yachts on the water, giant rulers in place of their masts.

A queen, complete with crown, frowning over a slate with 2 + 4 written on it.

A pupil, very neatly dressed in an old-fashioned school uniform, sitting at a desk.

The teacher floats up to the ceiling, and sticks to it.

A big squashy parcel on the wall.

A giant swelling raising the floor.

A pencil with a paintbrush end instead of an eraser end.

See what you can do with your suggested keywords.

CREATING GOOD KEYWORDS

There are several things to note about the words I've chosen. First of all, they are all nouns. Moreover, they are concrete, not abstract, nouns. That is, they are things that you can visualize.

Regal, for example, would be a great keyword for *regla*, except that you can't picture *regal* very well (you could of course picture a king or queen, or someone with great deportment, but would these images necessarily bring to mind the word *regal*? That's the deciding issue.)

Of course, it is not always possible to find an appropriate concrete noun — that's why sometimes you have to go with a sentence or phrase instead of a picture — but that's what you should be trying for first.

They are also all words that are familiar to me. That's where the individual comes in — what is a good word for me is not necessarily a good word for you.

You may, for example, find *regalia* a better word than *regatta*. If you're familiar with *lapis* (lazuli) as a gem or pigment, that would be a better word than *lapel*. If you're a birdwatcher, *swallow* would probably be a better word than *swelling*.

Note too, that I chose *queen* for *cuentas*. This goes back to what I said about acoustic similarity: although we don't usually think of c and q having the same sound, the sound cu in Spanish is the same as the English sound qu.

Effective keywords need to not only sound like the target word and be able to form memorable links with the meaning, they also need to be different from each other — you don't want to get confused between too-similar keywords. Where possible, they should also be concrete and familiar. (As I've said, you can have a concrete word that symbolizes an abstraction, such as an image of a blindfolded woman holding a pair of scales for *justice*. The crucial thing is that the symbol recalls, for you, the abstract noun.)

Perhaps most importantly of all — more important, research suggests, than distinctiveness, vividness, concreteness — is relational and semantic information. This is why the emphasis now is on making *interactive* images or sentences. It is not enough for the two images, the keyword and the meaning, to be in the same image; they must interact.

Thus we don't have a garage *and* a mountain, we have a garage *teetering on* a mountain. The pupil *sits at* the desk; the puppet *hangs out of* the wastepaper bin. The better (the more active; the more meaningful) the interactive connection, the more effective it will be.

The advantage of a semantic connection may be seen in the following example, taken from an experimental study[1]. Students in a free control condition (those told to use their own methods to remember) almost all used a keyword-type technique to learn some items. But unlike those in the keyword group, the keywords chosen by these subjects typically had some semantic connection as well.

Thus, for the Spanish word *pestana*, meaning *eyelash*, several people used the phrase *paste on* as a link, reflecting an existing association (pasting on false eyelashes). The keyword supplied to the keyword group, on the other hand, was *pest*, which has no obvious connection to eyelash. (It is also worth noting that verbal links were more commonly used by control subjects, rather than mental images.)

It seems likely that keywords that are semantically as well as acoustically related to the word to be learned will be remembered longer and more easily.

Relatedly, two studies[2] that compared the keyword strategy with learning by context (a popular strategy among teachers) found that the best method was one that combined both — that is, where students were given not only the keyword, but also example sentences, showing the word in context.

In other words, use of the keyword mnemonic should not

blind you to the value of seeking and attaching meaning. Creating meaningful links should always take precedence over arbitrary links, however vivid and distinctive.

Note too, that although it is usually recommended that you should try to create bizarre images, the research evidence for this is mixed[3]. Having bizarre images seems to help remembering immediately after learning only when there is a mix of bizarre and less unusual images, and may not particularly help over the long term at all.

It seems plausible that one reason for the conflicting experimental results is the fuzzy question of what exactly constitutes 'bizarreness'. It may be that some forms of peculiarity help memory, while others don't (and may even hinder it). It does seem clear, however, that most people find it harder to come up with bizarre images. Accordingly, I would recommend that you should only use bizarre images when they come easily to mind.

These, then, are the dimensions along which keywords can be evaluated for effectiveness:

- meaningfulness

- acoustic similarity

- imageability

- distinctiveness

- familiarity

The fact that I call these dimensions is a clue that keywords can, and will, vary considerably along these dimensions! In other words, you try the best you can, but sometimes you will have to accept keywords that measure poorly on these dimensions. That does not necessarily mean they will be ineffective.

For example, here are some keywords Atkinson & Raugh used in their study that were startlingly effective. For all of these the difference in recall between those learning in the keyword condition and the control condition was greater than 40% — for example, the probability that those in the keyword condition would remember that *dévushka* meant *girl* was 100% but only 50% for those in the control condition; the probability that those in the keyword condition would remember that *vózdux* meant *air* was 77% compared to 35% for those in the control condition.

Russian	Keyword	Meaning
DÉVUSHKA	[dear vooshka]	girl
VNIMÁNIE	[pneumonia]	attention
TARÉIKA	[daddy elk]	plate
KARANDÁSH	[car run dash]	pencil
EDÁ	[ya die]	food
VÓZDUX	[fuzz duke]	air

It cannot be said that these are good examples of keywords according to most of the dimensions I have described, and yet they worked very well. My own feeling is that these are clear examples of the importance, and effectiveness, of the verbal part of the imagery link (Atkinson & Raugh also called this the mnemonic link, and this is perhaps a better term in some ways). Nevertheless, the reason why these keywords were so effective is mysterious, and emphasizes that the guidelines are only that. They are not rules. Ultimately, a good keyword is one that works for you.

Having said that, a study[4] that used "good" keywords and "poor" ones showed not only that the quality of the keywords makes a significant difference, but that judges could accurately assess the memorability of keywords. So, as a general rule (inexplicable cases aside), you can probably usually tell whether a particular word will make a good keyword.

For example, if we look at all the words for which the difference in recall between those learning in the keyword condition and the control condition was greater than 40%, we also see: DVOR [divorce]; NACHÁLO [not shallow]; KUSÓK [blue sock]; NARÓD [narrow road]; TOLPÁ [tell pa]; GORÁ [garage]; GÁLSTUK [gallstone]; PLÓSHCHAD' [postage]; USLÓVIE [Yugoslavia]; DURÁK [two rocks]; ÓSEN' [ocean]; STRANÁ [strawman]; VÝXOD [boyhood]; ZHÁZHDA [judge]; GÓLOD [gullet].

Interestingly, the study found no particular disadvantage to using a keyword phrase — these were recalled about as well as single keywords.

Parts of speech are another matter.

In a later study by Atkinson & Raugh[5] in which verbs and adjectives were used as well as nouns, while nouns and verbs were remembered at about the same rate, adjectives were noticeably harder to remember. This could be related to the adjectives tending to be longer words, but it seems most likely it has with the greater difficulty in visualizing them.

Choosing a good keyword

A good keyword will sound as much as possible like the to-be-learned word.

A good keyword will easily form an interactive image with the word meaning.

A good keyword will be sufficiently unlike other keywords to not be confused.

A good keyword will be a familiar word, easily recalled.

Nouns and verbs are usually better than adjectives.

Is it all about good keywords? How important is the image?

Atkinson & Raugh explored these questions a little further by adding two groups — those who only learned the acoustic link, and those who only learned the imagery link. From this study it appears that both the acoustic link and the imagery link are important, and neither one is more important than the other. Moreover, the two links are independent — performance on one was unrelated to performance on the other.

But don't forget that the mnemonic link doesn't have to be an image. If a verbal link works better for you, that's fine — just remember that the crucial charactcristic is that it connects the keyword with its associated word in a way that is active and meaningful.

Crafting a good image

A good image will be simple.

A good image will tie the keyword with its associated word in a way that is *active* and personally *meaningful*.

A good image will be clear and vivid.

HOW EFFECTIVE IS THE KEYWORD METHOD?

The keyword mnemonic should not be regarded as a universal remedy. There was considerable variation among the 120 words to be learned, ranging from the 100% recall for *dévushka* to 27% recall for *lápa* (paw) — which was in fact remembered much better in the control condition (58%).

Nevertheless, over a third of the words were remembered over 80% of the time by those in the keyword condition, compared to only **one** item by those in the control condition (*glaz* for *eye* — a mnemonic link so obvious I am sure most of the control participants used it). Moreover, only seven words were remembered **less** than half the time in the keyword condition, compared to 70 in the control condition!

Overall, the keyword group recalled 72% of the words when they were tested on the day following the three study days (40 words were studied each day), compared to 46% by the control group. When they were (without warning) tested again six weeks later, the keyword group remembered 43% compared to the control group's 28%.

These statistics make a compelling case for the effectiveness of the keyword mnemonic over rote repetition. The precipitous drop in both cases at six weeks is entirely expected, and should be taken as a loud warning that you cannot expect *any* memory strategy to work without sufficient repetition. I discuss the best way of providing that in the final section.

It should also be noted that the control group was instructed to use any strategy they could think of to learn the words. Assuredly some of the participants used a keyword-type mnemonic at least some of the time — for example, in the case of *glaz* (eye), which was remembered 92% of the time by control subjects.

In comparison, in an earlier study[6] using Spanish words in which control subjects were specifically instructed to use rote repetition, the control group only scored 28% compared to the keyword group's 88% (decidedly higher than the 72% scored in the Russian study, perhaps reflecting how much easier it is to find good keywords, with Spanish being much more closely related to English).

One benefit the keyword method seems to grant is to make the imageability of the word-to-be-learned less important. For the control group, words of high imageability were learned better than words of low imageability, as we would expect. However, for those using the keyword method, the imageability of the words was not an issue — again, unsurprisingly once you think about it, because what the method has done is to create imageability where there is little.

But I'm not advocating total reliance on the keyword method. The first strategy in learning a new word should always be to look for a familiar root or cognate.

Spanish, for example, has many hundreds of common words that are very similar to English. It would be pointless to use the keyword mnemonic on such as those. Indeed, it's worth making an effort to look for roots even when they don't hit you in the face — they're not always obvious, but having found them they become more obvious, and are likely to help you remember the word. (Like many others I am pleased to have learned Latin at school, for the help that has given me in learning those languages that, like our own, includes many words that derive from Latin.)

Limitations of the keyword method

The keyword method is primarily a strategy for recognition learning. You see the word *carta*, the keyword *cart* is triggered, and hopefully the image of the letter in the cart is then recalled. The method is not so useful the other way around, for remembering the Spanish for *letter*.

The problem is, of course, that generating the unfamiliar word from the keyword is much harder than remembering the (familiar) keyword from the unfamiliar word — *go* from *górod* is easy; *górod* from *go* is much less so.

That's why the keyword method is only one of what should be several strategies that you need to employ in learning new words.

But being able to recognize words, to remember their meanings, is hugely useful. Doing that enables you to read more fluently; reading as much as you can is how you get the repetition you need to firmly embed the words (this is a much better form of repetition than rote repetition, because it's more interesting and more contextual). The advantage of the keyword method is that it gets the words into your head faster, enabling you to more easily get the practice you need.

Experimental research, of course, invariably involves very limited numbers of words to be learned. While this is entirely understandable, it does raise the question of the extent to which these findings are applicable to real world learning situations. If you are learning a new language, you are going to have to learn at least 2000 new words. Does the keyword mnemonic hold up in those circumstances?

While the keyword mnemonic has been used in real world situations (intensive language courses), these are not experimental situations, and we must be wary of the conclusions we draw from them. The keyword strategy does take time and effort to implement, and may well have disadvantages if used to excess. As I've discussed, some words lend themselves to other techniques. At least for more experienced students (who will have a number of effective strategies, and are capable of applying them appropriately) the keyword strategy is probably best used selectively.

Remembering for the long term

No one can deny the effectiveness of the keyword method for immediate recall; however, whether or not it is better for long-term recall (which is, after all, what most of us are after) has been a much more contentious issue[7].

While many studies have found good remembering a week or two after learning using the keyword mnemonic, others have found that remembering is no better than any other strategy one or two weeks later. Some have found it worse.

It has been suggested that, although the keyword may be a good retrieval cue initially, over time earlier associations regain their strength and make it harder to retrieve the keyword image. This seems very reasonable to me — any keyword is, by its nature, an easily retrieved, familiar word; therefore, it will already have a host of associations. When you're tested immediately after learning the keyword, this new link will of course be fresh in your mind and easily retrieved. But as time goes on, and the advantage of recency is lost, what is there to make the new link stronger than the other, existing, links? Absolutely nothing — unless you strengthen it. How? By repetition.

Notwithstanding Atkinson & Raugh's finding that the acoustic and the imagery links are equally important (and confirming the relative independence of these two links), over time it seems that it is not the keyword itself that is usually forgotten. It's the image.

This implies that the part of the mnemonic that you must particularly work on is the link between keyword and image. For example, the garage *on the mountain*. It's a natural impulse to put one's energies into strengthening *gorá – garage*, but your focus should be on putting that garage on the mountain.

I believe the reason why the keyword strategy has sometimes shown itself less effective when tested for long-term memory is the ease with which words are initially mastered. This encourages students to give up repeating them long before they have been truly fixed in memory. What you need to remember is that how long something is remembered for is not a matter of the method you used in learning it — what matters is how *well* you learned it.

It's often suggested that a mnemonic you've thought up yourself will be stronger than one that is given to you, but there is no evidence for this in relation to keywords. Indeed, much of the time students do better if they're given the keyword, rather than having to think it up themselves[8].

It seems likely that the inconsistency in results reflects the fact that whether or not it's better if you're given keywords or better to think them up yourself depends not on any specific rule but on how difficult it is to find an appropriate keyword and how skilled you are.

Similarly, whether or not it's better to see an actual visual image rather than simply have that image described to you, probably depends on the individual — I personally am much more verbal than visual, and I do find constructing an image from clipart helps me considerably. However, those who are good visualizers are less likely to need such assistance.

What is clear from the research is that instruction in the technique is vitally important. Indeed there is some evidence that effective use of the keyword mnemonic requires individual instruction (as opposed to group instruction). But I don't think this is the crucial ingredient to effective instruction. I think that the difference between experiments where the keyword mnemonic has been clearly superior, and those where it has not, comes down to how much direction the students have been given in how to use the technique.

Durable keyword images do require quite a lot of practice to create. It has been suggested that initially people tend to simply focus on creating distinctive images. It may only be with extensive practice that you become able to reliably create images that effectively *integrate* the relational qualities of the bits of information.

What all this suggests is that successful and continued use of the keyword mnemonic requires more instruction and practice than you might think.

Comparing the keyword mnemonic to other strategies

As a general rule, experimental studies into the effectiveness of the keyword mnemonic have compared it to rote repetition, or, less often, "trying your hardest to remember". It is not overwhelmingly surprising that the keyword mnemonic should be superior to rote repetition, and comparisons with "free" controls will often show inconsistent (and uninformative) results because some participants will be using the keyword method at least some of the time. For example, in one experimental study[9], 17 out of the 40 control subjects used the keyword method for at least some items, and many of the keyword subjects didn't always use the keyword method. For the control subjects, the probability of recalling keyword-elaborated items was 81% vs 45% for other items, while for the keyword group, the probability of recall for keyword-elaborated items was 80% vs 16% for those items for which they didn't use a keyword mnemonic.

While this certainly emphasizes that the keyword mnemonic is hugely more effective than rote repetition, it doesn't tell us how the keyword method compares with other effective (or presumed to be effective) strategies.

A number of studies[10] have compared the keyword strategy against the context method of learning vocabulary (a method much loved by teachers — students experience the word to be learned in several different meaningful contexts). Theory suggests that the context method should encourage multiple connections to the target word, and so it's expected to be a highly effective strategy.

However, the studies have found that the keyword method produces better learning than the context method, including when the students had to work out the meaning of the word themselves, from the context.

This was true even when subjects were given a test that would be thought to give an advantage to the context method — namely, subjects being required to produce meaningful sentences with the target words.

But it seems likely that all this depends on the student and her background knowledge. All these strategies — using context, finding roots and synonyms/antonyms, generating meaningful sentences — are elaboration strategies. It would not be surprising if, as with elaborative interrogation, these strategies require a certain level of knowledge and understanding to be used effectively. The crucial thing about mnemonics is that they are the best strategy when such knowledge and understanding is lacking.

WHEN THE KEYWORD METHOD IS USEFUL

As I said before, it is not only for learning another language that the keyword mnemonic is useful. It is also an excellent strategy for learning new technical vocabulary.

Remember when I talked about the common medical mnemonic for the cranial nerves (**O**n **O**ld **O**lympia's **T**owering **T**op **A F**inn **A**nd **G**erman **V**ault **A**nd **H**op), I mentioned the problem of remembering the names of the nerves: olfactory, optic, oculomotor, trochlear, trigeminal, abducens, facial, auditory, glossopharyngeal, vagus, accessory, and hypoglossal. Several of these are familiar words, but the rest certainly need something to make them more memorable! See if you can come up with good keywords for them.

oculomotor	
trochlear	
trigeminal	
abducens	
glossopharyngeal	
vagus	
hypoglossal	

We will return to this mnemonic when we look at the pegword method.

Using the keyword mnemonic to remember gender

One other aspect of vocabulary learning for many languages is that of gender. The keyword mnemonic has successfully been used to remember the gender of nouns, by incorporating a gender tag into the image[11]. This may be as simple as including a man or a woman (or some particular object, when the language also contains a neutral gender), or you could use some other code — for example, if learning German, you could use the image of a deer for the masculine gender (*der*), the iconic image of Death with a sickle or a single die (plural dice) for the feminine gender (*die*).

Non-European languages

The use of the keyword method in learning vocabulary is obvious when the vocabulary is in a related language; its use between unrelated languages that don't use the same script is much less obvious. Intriguingly, some Chinese researchers have tackled this problem for Chinese learning English[12].

Their solution is to devise an intermediary code, by which every letter in the alphabet is linked to a specific Chinese character that has some phonetic or graphic link to the letter. These associations must, of course, be extremely well learned.

Having over-learned these, the student then goes on to learn what the researchers call the basic key-letters method, which is used only with English words 2-3 letters long. In this, both the letters in a 2-letter word, and the last 2 letters in a 3-letter word, are transformed into their Chinese character counterparts. The meaning of these characters is then integrated into an image or sentence incorporating the meaning of the English word. Once this basic method has been mastered, the student can extend the method to longer words.

The study, involving a group of junior high school students (all of whom were reported as possibly learning disabled), was remarkably successful in improving their learning of English words.

In the next, brief, chapter, we will look at further extensions of the keyword method.

Main points to remember

Keywords provide artificial meaning when words can't be meaningfully connected.

Practice should focus on the mnemonic link (usually an image) rather than the keyword itself.

The keyword method is mainly a recognition strategy.

The keyword method is an effective strategy for learning words fast.

Don't let quick fluency fool you into thinking you have learned a specific keyword mnemonic — long-term learning requires repeated review over time.

Extensions of the keyword method

MORE THAN WORDS

The keyword method was originally designed for the learning of foreign languages, and most of its educational use beyond that has involved its use in specialist topics — learning technical words and concepts in science and social studies. However the technique can be extended to any associated pairs.

For example, one study[1] used a modified keyword method to teach 4th and 5th graders the U.S. states and their capitals. Each state and each capital were given keywords (e.g., marry for Maryland; apple for Annapolis), and these keywords were linked in a captioned picture ("The capital of Maryland is Annapolis. Here is a picture of two apples getting married").

Because they would ultimately need to recall the capital on seeing the state's name, when learning the capitals the students practiced recalling the capital from the keyword, rather than the other way around. They were taught 12 capital-state pairs using this method, then on the following day they were given 13 new pairs and told to learn them any way they wished. When tested two days later, an average of 71.2% of the keyword-learned pairs were correctly recalled, compared to 36.4% of the control pairs — in other words, around twice as many were recalled using the keyword method.

You could also extend this technique to such associated pairs as the authors of particular books. For example, to remember that Luigi Pirandello wrote *Six Characters in Search of an Author*, you could visualize *piranha* tearing apart *six carrots*. To remember Joseph Conrad wrote *Heart of Darkness*, you could visualize a *con*vict eating a *black heart*. To remember Anton Chekhov wrote *Uncle Vanya*, you could visualize your *uncle* with a *van* tattooed on his *cheek*.

APPLYING THE KEYWORD METHOD TO TEXT

A few studies[2] have extended the keyword method to text, mainly to short biographical passages. For example, to remember that a (fictional) person called Charlene McKune was famous for having a counting cat, the name 'McKune' is given the keyword *raccoon*, and an interactive image is constructed combining the counting cat with the raccoon (say, a cat counting raccoons jumping over a fence).

These studies have shown that the keyword method can be an effective strategy for short text. But another study[3] shows that some ways of applying the strategy are better than others. This study, involving 160 university students, was looking at ways of reducing interference between similar bits of information — for example, the causes of the American Revolutionary War and the War of 1812.

In 'ordinary' learning, interference is reduced if there's a significant gap (at least a day) between reading the similar passages. It can also be reduced if you can connect the separate passages to existing knowledge (that's why experts are much less prone to interference when acquiring new information). However, if you had that degree of knowledge in the topic, you wouldn't need to be looking at mnemonics! So it's good to know that mnemonics can also help you minimize interference.

The study used biographical passages that contained 11 pieces of concrete, easily visualizable facts, presented in separate sentences. One group of students was taught a single image integrating all 11 keywords for each passage; another was given 11 separate images (there were also two other control groups, one of whom was given passages that were completely dissimilar).

Here's an example from the study (keywords italicized).

Separate images:

a *RACCOON* waving from an *apartment* doorway

a RACCOON riding a toy *train*

a *RACCOON* talking to a *parrot*

a *RACCOON* throwing *newspapers* onto a doorstep

a *RACCOON* strumming a *guitar*

a *RACCOON* saluting a *soldier*

a *RACCOON* driving a *truck*

a *RACCOON* sucking on a piece of *candy*

a *RACCOON* swinging a *tennis* racquet

a *RACCOON* lying in a pile of broken *pottery*

a *RACCOON* hiking through a *desert*

The integrated image:

a huge *RACCOON* waving from an *apartment* doorway to a parrot riding a toy train and throwing *newspapers* to a *soldier* who is strumming a *guitar* while driving a *truck* loaded with *candy* that has run over a *tennis* player now lying in a pile of broken *pottery* painted with *desert* scenes.

The integrated mnemonic produced as little interference as the control group given dissimilar texts, and significantly better memory than the separate mnemonics (an average 86.1% correct recall compared to 65.7% for the separate mnemonics, and 68.9% for the control using the same texts). As can be surmised from these figures, the separate mnemonics produced as much interference as the control group using the same texts.

All this would seem to be clear evidence that a single integrated mnemonic should be used for related information. However it should be noted that a previous study[4] by these researchers found that separate mnemonics were as effective as an integrated mnemonic when students were asked to learn four 5-sentence biographies. It may be that separate mnemonics are adequate when the number of facts is low.

But it may also reflect how the mnemonics were constructed. In the study where no difference was found, the integrated image was built up bit by bit, one sentence at a time. In the later study, where the integrated image was more successful, the whole passage was presented, and the integrated image shown, in its entirety, at the end.

This seems to suggest that it is better to create a single, integrated mnemonics for related information from text, and to create it as a whole once you have gathered all the information.

Here's another, more naturalistic example of applying the keyword method to text. In this study[5], college students applied the strategy to a 1,800-word passage about historical theories of human intelligence.

The text involved two sub-topics: measurement of intelligence, and structure of intelligence. The former included information about five theorists, and the latter seven theorists. The "free-study" group were given a written summary after each paragraph, highlighting each theorist's major contributions. The mnemonic group were given a keyword for each theorist's name and, after each paragraph, a drawing connecting the keyword with major aspects of the theory (a written description of the picture was also supplied).

So, for example, the paragraph on Alfred Binet was followed by a drawing in which a *crowd* (*crowd* was used to signify the measurement subtopic; a *single person* signified the structure subtopic) watched a man in a racing car wearing a *bonnet*. Under the drawing were the words <u>Binet</u> – <u>bonnet</u>, followed by the text: "This race-car driver is competing in a race while wearing a special <u>bonnet</u> to protect his brain, to remind us of the fact that <u>Binet</u> believed higher mental processes existed and should be measured."

Similarly, the drawing for Spearman showed a *single man* holding a "primary" *spear*, with several specialized ones on the ground, signifying Spearman's theory of general-plus-specific abilities.

Students were tested by writing brief essays, followed by a matching task in which they matched the name with various facts.

Those using the mnemonic technique performed significantly better (more than twice as well) at matching the theorist with the major facts, and about the same as the free-study group at matching them with other, incidental facts. They also did better at knowing the temporal order, although that was not something explicitly emphasized.

Moreover, it is noteworthy that both groups showed the same level of structural coherence in their essays. Mnemonic techniques have been criticized for "cluttering" the mind with unconnected facts. This finding counters that criticism.

As in the case of the state-capitals, it pays to think about what your retrieval cues are likely to be. You'll remember that in the last chapter I talked about the problem of backward recall — the fact that it is easier to derive the keyword from the target word (*go* from *górod*), than to derive the target word from the keyword (*górod* from *go*). With the capitals, the students practiced recalling the capital from the keyword in order to overcome this problem.

Similarly, when you're constructing a multi-item mnemonic, you should consider what the retrieval cue is likely to be.

In the study just described, for example, it was assumed the theorists' names (Binet, Spearman, etc) would be given. The student would then retrieve the keyword from the name, and the keyword would trigger the associated image with the rest of the information.

However, it is quite likely that in normal circumstances you would have to recall the theorists' names having been given some general cue, such as "famous psychologists who contributed to the measurement of intelligence". In other words, it is the concept of *measurement of intelligence* that will be the cue, and it is the link between this concept and its keyword that you'd need to practice (as well, of course, as the image linked to the keyword).

Main points to remember

The keyword method can be used for any associated pairs, such as capitals of countries or authors of books.

The keyword method can also be used for several items of related information, such as the main points in a text.

If using the keyword method to remember several items of related information, you should aim to create one single integrated mnemonic.

When practicing your mnemonic, think about what your retrieval cue will be.

THE FACE-NAME MNEMONIC

You probably haven't thought about this mnemonic as one applicable to study tasks, although you may well be familiar with it. The face-name association method is one of the more commonly used mnemonics, and it is an extension of the keyword method.

You begin by selecting a distinctive feature of a face and searching for a word or phrase that is acoustically similar to the person's name. You then create an interactive image linking the feature with the keyword.

This mnemonic is of course mostly used to help people with that most-important everyday task of remembering people's names. However, the method has applications beyond that.

Carney & Levin[6] have explored using this mnemonic to help art appreciation students remember which artists painted what paintings.

Applying the face-name mnemonic to art & artists

The application of the face-name technique to paintings (or indeed other artwork) is readily apparent:

1. Select a distinctive and prominent element in the painting.

2. Search for an acoustically similar word to the artist's name.

3. Create an interactive image (or sentence) connecting the keyword to the element.

Thus, for the famous painting of "Gilles", a clown in a baggy white suit, by Watteau, you could imagine the clown carrying buckets of water, with water pouring down on him from above (example from Carney & Levin 2000; for a link to an image of this and the Rouault painting mentioned below, go to the book resources on my website). To remember that Monet painted "Water lilies", you could imagine money raining down on, and being gathered up into, a giant waterlily.

This in itself is a very helpful application, but the really intriguing extension is what the researchers did next.

Knowing the artist when you see a particular painting that you have studied is one thing, but even better is seeing a painting you've never studied, and knowing who the artist probably is. That is, being able to recognize an artist's style.

Carney & Levin compared students' performance on remembering the artist of a painting they'd seen before, and correctly attaching an artist to paintings they hadn't seen before, according to four different training instructions. Half the students were told to use their own methods, and half were trained with the mnemonic. However, half of the mnemonic group were told to select something distinctive about the style or theme of the artist, rather than a specific detail in the painting.

For example, for the painting *This Will be the Last Time, Little Father!* by Georges Rouault, the mnemonic-detail group focused on the skeleton, creating an image of the skeleton's ribs being played on with a ruler (keyword for Rouault). The mnemonic-general group, however, focused on the heavy dark lines that are characteristic of Rouault's work, and imagined making heavy dark lines with a ruler dipped in black paint. Similarly, half the control ("use your own best method") group was told to focus on the general theme or style (e.g., "heavy, dark lines").

The results were very clear. Despite being told to focus on the style, the control-general students were little better than the control-detail students at recognizing new paintings (an average of just over 50% compared to 44%). The mnemonic-general students, however, were clear winners (an average of 73% correct). (The mnemonic-detail students scored just under 52% — that is, no better than the control-detail students.)

Moreover, the mnemonic-general group still scored very well on the specific paintings they had studied (90% compared to 99% for the mnemonic-detail group, 73% for the control-detail, and nearly 67% for the control-general).

Applying the face-name mnemonic to animals

A further study[7] by these researchers used this technique to remember the names of animals. For example, the animal *capybara* was given the keyword *cap* and students were told to "Imagine this flat-headed animal with a cap (capybara) pulled down low over its eyes!". Similarly, a long-tailed lizard called a basilisk could be given the keyword *basket*, and an image could be formed in which the lizard is in a small basket, its long tail draped over the side.

Again, the students using the mnemonic performed significantly better than those using their own methods.

This is a useful application for those studying zoology, and indicates further extension to other organisms, for example, plants and even microscopic creatures. Indeed, the researchers suggest the technique could be extended to identifying countries from their outlines, recognizing parts of the body, minerals, and different kinds of dinosaurs.

Extending the mnemonic to taxonomic & attribute information

In an extension of a similar study[8], in which students were taught to distinguish and name different fish species, the students were also given some hierarchical (taxonomic) information about the fish. For example, "The order <u>Scorpaeniformes</u> includes the family <u>Triglidae</u>, which in turn includes the two fish species, <u>Gurnard</u> and <u>Robin</u>."

Those in the mnemonic condition were told to "Imagine that a <u>scorpion</u> has a hold of a <u>tiger</u>. The tiger leaps down toward a <u>guard</u> who is guarding a <u>robin</u>." There was also a picture illustrating this.

The mnemonic group again significantly out-performed the control group, on matching the fish to the name (89% vs 76%), on identifying the fish (88.5% vs 60%), on filling in blank hierarchical arrangements (80% vs 37%), and on an analogy test of students' ability to infer hierarchical fish-classifications and relationships (77% vs 48%).

Similarly, a study with 8th-grade students[9] demonstrated the effectiveness of this kind of mnemonic for remembering the attributes of minerals. The students were given information about nine different minerals, and their attributes on three dimensions: hard/soft, pale/dark, home use/industrial use. Those in the mnemonic condition were given, in addition to this information, keywords for each mineral name, iconic images for each attribute, and a drawing combining all these. Thus, *hard* was represented by an old man, and *soft* by a baby; *dark* by a mean dark cat, and *pale* by a friendly pale cat; *home use* by a living room, and *industrial use* by a factory. The drawing for the mineral wolframite showed a baby hiding from a mean dark cat riding a wolf in a living room.

Tellingly, however, the group that saw all this in a picture performed not only significantly better than the group using their own method, but also significantly better than the group given the keywords and iconic images but not shown the illustration or given any description of it (they were simply told to "form a picture in your mind" drawing all these things together).

Does this mean that it's not enough to mentally visualize such complex images? Perhaps. But it may be that the students simply lacked sufficient training to use the mnemonic effectively without more support (and remember these were children). And again, of course, it surely depends on the individual's visualization abilities.

These two examples are similar to the examples of learning from text, in that both involve the construction of multi-item integrated images. It seems likely that creating such complex mnemonics does require considerable more practice than the simpler technique applied to associated pairs.

Main points to remember

The face-name association method can be used to encode visual information such as artwork, and animals.

The face-name association method and keyword method can be combined to form complex mnemonics.

Complex mnemonics integrating several bits of information do require a lot of practice.

Don't forget to think about what your retrieval cue will be!

Part III
List Mnemonics

Mnemonics for lists encompass almost all the complex mnemonic strategies after the keyword method (which is however a crucial component of these list-mnemonics).

Although shopping lists are always mentioned in the context of these strategies, and the "classic" list mnemonic (the method of loci, place or journey method) was developed primarily to help politicians remember their speeches, list mnemonics can also be usefully applied to study situations.

Ordered information, such as the top ten longest rivers, or the steps in a sequence, are obvious candidates. But list mnemonics can also help you remember the main points of a text. Even though this information is, presumably, meaningfully connected, when you are still building up your knowledge in the area it may well be that you lack sufficiently deep understanding to rely on that for memory. Or it may be that, although you understand it well enough, you need to be able to repeat with reasonable fidelity exactly what this particular text says. In other words, although you might know all the individual bits of information well enough, you might need help in ensuring that each one is tied firmly to the next one.

Furthermore, for those of you who have read *The Memory Key* or *Perfect Memory Training*, and remember the emphasis I put on anchors, those key bits of information that serve as reference points for a cluster (a small network of tightly connected information), list mnemonics can help you remember the anchors until your own developing understanding renders them unnecessary.

This is a point I would like to emphasize: building understanding requires time, and in the initial stages there is a lot that needs to be firmly tamped into your brain, before you truly, deeply, understand it. Mnemonics can help you at this stage. Don't worry about filling your head with meaningless, arbitrary connections, or that these might stand in the way of you developing true understanding. Mnemonics are merely a crutch that soon fades, once you have the information properly stored.

There are two main kinds of textual material for which mnemonic strategies are particularly appropriate:

- text that is readily understandable but which contains a number of details that might be overlooked

- text that is structured, but is not sufficiently well-known or well-organized for the structure to be used as a frame for retrieval

For your anchors you should select details you suspect you wouldn't otherwise remember, or details that would serve as effective cues for other bits of information. You encode those details by creating a visual image for them, and then integrate the details using the list-learning mnemonic.

To use a list-learning strategy for text

<u>Select</u> the anchors.

<u>Encode</u> the anchors (keyword mnemonic).

<u>Cluster</u> the encoded anchors (list mnemonic).

Let's look at the various list-mnemonics.

The story method

The story method (sometimes called the sentence mnemonic) is the most easily learned list-mnemonic strategy, although not as widely known as the other simple methods we've talked about so far.

As its name suggests, the story method involves linking words to be learned in a story. While this is most obviously useful for learning actual lists, it can also be used for remembering the main points of a passage. In such a case, you need to reduce each point to a single word, which hopefully has the power to recall the whole point.

EXAMPLES

Remembering word lists

Let's look at an example. First, an easy one — a list:

Vegetable Instrument College Carrot Nail Fence Basin Merchant Scale Goat

This can be transformed into:

A VEGETABLE can be a useful INSTRUMENT for a COLLEGE student. A CARROT can be a NAIL for your FENCE or BASIN. But a MERCHANT would SCALE that fence and feed the carrot to a GOAT.

But let's face it, this is not a very probable list of words for you to memorize. The example is taken (with some modification) from a laboratory experiment[1], and the few tests of the story mnemonic that there have been have tended to involve such lists of unrelated words. But learning lists of unrelated words is not something we need to do very often. And generally, if we do have lists of words to learn — say, the names of the elements in the periodic table — they're going to be too technical to lend themselves readily to creating a story.

Even if the words themselves are not particularly technical, the nature of them is not likely to lend itself to a narrative. Let me show you what I mean. Consider the taxonomy of living things:

Kingdom

Phylum

Class

Order

Family

Genus

Species

Here's an attempt at a story:

In the KINGDOM, PHYLUM is a matter of CLASS, but ORDER is a matter for FAMILY, and GENIUS lies in SPECIES.

The trouble with this is not the re-coding of *genus* to *genius*; the trouble is, it doesn't make a lot of sense. It's a sentence, but not a story — there's no narrative. Humans think in stories. We find them easy to remember because they fit in with how we think. It follows then that the more effective story mnemonics will actually tell a story. To do that, we're going to have to transform our technical words into more common words.

King Phillip went to the **classroom** to **order** the **family genius** to **specifically** name the individual who had stolen the taxi.

The last part of this is of course unnecessary — you could finish it after individual if you wished. But an important thing to remember is that it's not about brevity. It's about memorability. And memorability is not as much affected by amount to remember, as it is by the details of what is being remembered. So meaningfulness is really important. Adding that little detail about stealing the taxi adds meaningfulness (and also underlines what this mnemonic is about: taxonomy).

Here's a longer example. Remember our hard-to-remember cranial nerves? This story was mentioned in a 1973 *Psychology Today* article by the eminent psychologist G.H. Bower[2]:

At the **oil factory** the **optician** looked for the **occupant** of the **truck**. He was searching because **three gems** had been **abducted** by a man who was hiding his **face** and **ears**. A **glossy photograph** had been taken of him, but it was too **vague** to use. He appeared to be **spineless** and **hypocritical**.

Here it is again with the nerves shown for comparison:

At the **oil factory** (olfactory) the **optician** (optic) looked for the **occupant** (oculomotor) of the **truck** (trochlear). He was searching because **three gems** (trigeminal) had been **abducted** (abducens) by a man who was hiding his **face** (facial) and **ears** (auditory). A **glossy photograph** (glossopharyngeal) had been taken of him, but it was too **vague** (vagus) to use. He appeared to be **spineless** (spinal accessory) and **hypocritical** (hypoglossal).

Notice how, with these technical words, they have been transformed into more familiar words — this is what I meant by saying the keyword method is a vital part of all these list-mnemonics.

Remembering text

Let's try something completely different. Here's a selection of points from articles in my local newspaper that I want to remember to tell my partner: council promises support for replacement of the fire-damaged local surf lifesaving clubhouse; council calls for comments about proposal to open a pedestrian mall to buses; daylight saving marks the start of beach restrictions for dogs; Playcentre Federation calls for government support for more parent education classes; robot exhibition coming soon; organizers of eDay (for recycling computer equipment) given award; secondary schools choir to sing at cathedral.

The first thing to do is choose a keyword / phrase to represent each item: burnt house, bus, dog, parent class, robot, computers, cathedral.

Now I need to construct a story. A big advantage I have in this case is that the order is not important, which helps a lot. So I can say:

The **robot** walked out of the **burnt house**, carrying a **broken computer**. Barking, the **dog** herded him onto a **bus**, which took them both to the **cathedral**, where a group of **parents** were having a **class** on computer trauma.

Once again, there are elaborative details which serve no purpose but to make the story more memorable: that the dog is barking; that the class is about computer trauma.

Where possible, you should always try and select concrete keywords — ones that are easy to visualize (even though this is a verbal rather than a visual strategy).

Let's try something a little more abstract. Say you're Scott Atran giving a speech on the genesis of suicide terrorism (taken from an article by Scott Atran, published in *Science*, and reproduced in *The Best American Science and Nature Writing 2004*). Here are the main points you want to cover:

> Definition (freedom fighters; French Resistance; Nicaraguan Contras; US Congress, act; two official definitions; restriction to suicide terrorism)

> History (Zealots; hashashin; French Revolution; 20th century revolutions; kamikaze; Middle East – 1981 Beirut; Hezbollah; Hamas; PIJ; Al-Qaida - Soviet-Afghan War; fundamentalism error)

> Difficulties of defending against (many targets, many attackers, low cost, detection difficulty; prevention)

> Explaining why (insults; attribution error;

Milgram; perceived contexts; interpretation)

Poverty link (crime – property vs violent; education; loss of advantage)

Institutions (unattached young males, normal, personal identity – Palestinians, Bosnians; peer loyalty; emotional manipulation)

Benefits (to individuals, to leaders, to organizations; effect of retaliation)

Prevention strategies (searches; moles; education; community pressure; need for research)

Rather than coming up with concrete keywords, let's try these main terms as they appear:

Toynbee's **definition** of **history fails** because it doesn't **explain why poverty** is dangerous, how **institutions benefit** young men, and how to **prevent** poor young men making history.

Toynbee (a famous historian) was chosen because we always remember things better if they involve an agent — thus ascribing the definition to a person is better than saying 'the best definition' or some such phrase.

The trouble with this is that it is not in itself particularly memorable: it doesn't really tell a story, again it's simply a coherent sentence. Worse than that, it's an abstract sentence. Let's try again, substituting our abstract words for more concrete terms:

Taking my **dictionary** in one hand and the **history** book in the other, I **defended** myself fiercely against the **wine** being hurled by the **Franciscan monk** as I passed by the **church**. The building gave him the **advantage** of height and protection, and throwing my books at him only infuriated him. I searched for something else to **protect** myself with.

I tested this out by trying to recall my little story some hours later. I had no problem with the first part; I had to think a little to recall "advantage", and I had to really search for "protect". (I also tried to recall my first, abstract, sentence — this was much harder, and in fact I couldn't get past "explain why poverty".)

Let's try substituting our last two, abstract, words:

Taking my **dictionary** in one hand and the **history** book in the other, I **defended** myself fiercely against the **wine** being hurled by the **Franciscan monk** as I passed by the **church**. But **Benedict Arnold** joined him, throwing **condoms** at me.

If you know anyone called Benedict (or Bennie or Ben), that would be better. Or you could use benefactor, though it would help if you have a specific person in mind, who you immediately associate with benefactor. Condoms, of course, represent prevention / protection.

This of course only represents the main headings, the outline of the speech. To remember the points within each heading, you construct a separate story (or different mnemonic) for each one.

Thus, your chain linking freedom fighters; French Resistance; Nicaraguan Contras; US Congress, act; two official definitions; restriction to suicide terrorism, will begin with your dictionary. It's better to construct these separately for several reasons:

- it will be a very lengthy story if you include all the details in one story;

- if you lose your way, your outline and the other stories will be unaffected;

- it's easier to recover if you get derailed by questions.

As a guideline, there is some evidence$_3$ that there is little benefit from using the mnemonic for nine or more items.

PROS & CONS OF THE STORY METHOD

There are several points I want to make about the story method. First, it is a strategy that is easily learned.

Reflecting this, a study$_4$ involving 65 older adults (average age 67 years) found that the story method was initially of greater benefit than the loci method (a more complex mnemonic involving visual imagery, which we will look at in a later chapter).

However, with more practice, the loci method produced superior results. Interestingly, at the end of the training, when they were permitted to choose which of these two methods they wanted to use to learn the last items, more than twice as many chose the loci method. Even more tellingly, those who chose the loci method were the more expert in mnemonics.

These findings point not only to the fact that the story

method is easier to learn, but also that it is less powerful. This is not surprising — as a general rule, choosing a mnemonic strategy is a matter of trade-offs. You need to consider how much effort you're prepared to put in; how difficult the material is to learn; how much you have to learn. The more powerful strategies require more effort to master than the simple mnemonics we've been considering so far; it's only worth putting the effort in if you have a large amount of material that needs such effort.

You may be thinking that the reason why the story method is less powerful is that it is a verbal rather than a visual strategy. However, the story method has a direct counterpart among visual imagery techniques (the link method). A comparison of the two methods[5] found that although the imagery method resulted in better recall when people were tested immediately after learning, there was no difference after a week.

Although the story method is not as powerful as some other, more complex, mnemonic strategies, it's still an effective one. A comparison of the story method with three other learning strategies[6] found that although there was no difference in remembering immediately after learning, when tested a week later students who used the story method recalled the most. The benefit was even greater when they were tested two months after the initial learning experience.

The other methods were simple repetition, first-letter mnemonic, and category clustering. It's worth noting that at one week there was no significant difference in recall between those who used the first-letter mnemonic and those who used repetition. Category clustering was however of significant benefit. The researchers surmised that the reason category clustering didn't maintain its advantage was that the words to be learned were not particularly appropriate for such a technique, being largely unrelated.

This is a reminder that it is not simply about finding effective strategies — it's about matching effective strategies to the appropriate tasks / material.

An effective story mnemonic

- tells a meaningful story

- uses familiar, preferably imageable, words

- includes elaborative details that help memorability

- is not too long (fewer than 9 items)

The place method

The place method (or journey method, or method of loci) is the classic mnemonic strategy, having its first recorded use 2500 years ago (the traditional story of its origins involves feasting warriors, a collapsed roof, and a bard who can name the dead by remembering where everyone was sitting).

First of all, you choose a place you know extremely well. You might use a familiar route, your house, or a particular room in it. The crucial thing is that you can easily call to mind various 'landmarks' (different fixed objects in a room, for example, or different buildings on a route). These landmarks are your anchors. You must train yourself to go around your landmarks in a particular order. With a route of course, that is easy.

To remember a list, you simply imagine each item in turn at these landmarks. For example, a loaf of bread on the couch; a giant apple on the coffee table; the sink full of carrots; a giant banana in the bath, etc.

As with all mnemonics, you have to try it to appreciate that it really does work! The critical thing is to make sure you know your set of landmarks very well. That is, that you can close your eyes and clearly mentally visualize the places you are walking through. You then clearly, vividly, visualize the items you want to remember in those places. How well this strategy works for you does depend on your ability to make mental images.

But if you think you're not very good at this, remember what I said earlier: most people are better than they think, and it is a skill that improves with practice.

Like most mnemonic strategies, you can apply this strategy at different levels of expertise. At a basic level, it is quite easily learned, as long as you have a familiar place that you know in sufficient detail.

That may not be as easy as it sounds. It's quite amazing how unobservant we are! You may have trouble even with your own home, depending on how long you've lived there, how often you've moved, how often you re-arrange or change the furniture, etc.

So the first determinant of whether this is an easy strategy for you is how well you know suitable places. The second determinant is how good your visualization abilities are — this really is a visual strategy, not one that has a verbal counterpart or significant component.

USING THE PLACE METHOD

Assuming this is a good strategy for you, the next issue is when to use it. Shopping lists are all very well, but personally I'm just as happy writing things down on the back of an old envelope.

Unlike shopping lists, most lists are more abstract — which means they're harder to visualize, and since this is a purely visual strategy, you must have concrete (i.e., imageable) items. This means you have to transform your abstract items into concrete ones. But we have seen, in the discussion of the keyword mnemonic, how this can be done.

Moreover, not all your lists or texts will be abstract. Literature is usually grounded in visual images. Here, for example, is a brief text from Shakespeare:

> There is a tide in the affairs of men,
>
> Which, taken at the flood, leads on to fortune;
>
> Omitted, all the voyage of their life
>
> Is bound in shallows and in miseries.
>
> On such a full sea are we now afloat,
>
> And we must take the current when it serves,
>
> Or lose our ventures.
>
> Julius Caesar, IV. iii. 217

Let's dismember it into concrete images:

> tide: a rising tide
>
> affairs of men: male lovers
>
> flood

fortune: a pile of gold

omitted: an oven mitt

voyage: ship

shallows and in miseries: puddles, person weeping

On such a full sea are we now afloat: middle of the ocean, ship sailing serenely

Current: currant (the dried fruit)

lose our ventures: vultures flying away.

And now we place these images in their places:

- Open the front door, and there's a tidal wave coming in.

- On the inside couch are two males entwined.

- Water floods over the coffee table.

- The second couch is covered in a pile of gold.

- An oven mitt lies on the dining table.

- A toy boat sits on the fridge.

- There are puddles on the stove.

- A child sits on the microwave, crying.

- Another toy boat sails in the sink full of water.

- A giant currant sits on the TV.

- A vulture stands on the closet, wings out, ready to fly away.

Here's another example. Remember Atran's speech on terrorism? This was the story I came up with:

Taking my **dictionary** in one hand and the **history** book in the other, I **defended** myself fiercely against the **wine** being hurled by the **Franciscan monk** as I passed by the **church**. But **Benedict Arnold** joined him, throwing **condoms** at me.

We can express this same information using the method of loci:

- On the front door step there's a dictionary.

- On the inside couch there's a history book.

- The coffee table is covered by a shield.

- There's a bottle of wine on the second couch.

- A Franciscan monk is sitting at the dining table.

- A model church sits on the fridge.

- Benedict Arnold is working at the stove.

- The microwave is covered in condoms.

Some advice from antiquity

As mentioned, the place method dates back to antiquity. The principal instruction manual (an anonymous Roman text known as *Ad C. Herennium libri IV* , dated at 86 B.C.E.) gave the following advice regarding its use:

- To help make sure you haven't gone astray in your order, give every 5th and 10th place a distinguishing mark.

- A rarely frequented place is better, because crowds of passing people tend to interfere with the memory.

- The places shouldn't be too similar to each other, otherwise you're likely to get confused.

- The places shouldn't be too large (which makes the images attached to them vague) or too small (the images will be overcrowded).

- The places shouldn't be too brightly lit (which will make the images dazzling) or too poorly lit (which will make the images hard to see).

- The intervals between places shouldn't be too small or too large — they suggest 30 feet.

Modern research[1] adds to these recommendations the suggestion that the best routes are circular. These seem to reduce serial position effects (first and last items in a list are usually better remembered).

These instructions are surprising in the extent to which they specify the visual characteristics of the places that are, after all, to be used in your imagination. But despite this, it is not required that these places actually exist — places that exist only in your imagination are equally acceptable, as long as you can visualize them sufficiently well (these instructions point to how well that needs to be!). Indeed, Dante's Inferno supposedly described the circles of hell in such vivid detail so that they might serve as places that could be used in this way. In modern times, video games might provide such mnemonic places for some.

There is no denying that this method is one that requires far more training and practice than the other methods I have described so far. You need to not only be well-versed in your particular route (or routes — if you are serious about using this method, you'll find it useful to have several different routes), but also in forming the images that you place on the loci.

Moreover (and this is true for all the list-mnemonics), if you're going to use the method to help you remember important points in a text, you need to become skilled in identifying words in the text that provide good cues.

Effective loci

- are very well-known

- form a clear, circular route

- are sufficiently dissimilar from each other not to be confused

- are moderately, and reasonably evenly, spaced

- are visualized in clear lighting

- provide sufficient area for the arrangement of items

WHEN TO USE THE PLACE METHOD

In Roman times, this method was popularised as a strategy for helping people remember speeches (remember that classical cultures were predominantly oral; rhetoric was a highly prized skill). This is indeed one of the tasks for which this method is most suitable, because its purely visual nature enables you to hold it in your mind simultaneously as you speak — visuospatial working memory is separate from auditory/verbal working memory. So this method is an excellent choice if you are giving an oral presentation.

It's also a good choice if you want to remember main points for exam essays — particularly if you suffer from exam anxiety, where your brain freezes up. All mnemonics are good for that, but it may be that a visual strategy might be particularly effective, given that your exam block is rooted in verbal information.

Interestingly, a test$_2$ of the effectiveness of the method with different kinds of text found that the method was most effective with expository text (compared to descriptive and narrative passages — there was no difference between these in terms of performance). However, this was only significantly true when the texts were *heard*, rather than read (although performance on written expository text was better, it did not reach statistical significance).

In general, recall was higher, and more affected by passage type and mnemonic method, when the texts were presented orally.

For example, the highest average recall was 33.5% (achieved by using subject-generated loci on an expository passage), and the lowest average recall was 14.9% (from using verbal rehearsal on a narrative passage). The highest average recall when the texts were written was 30.6% (achieved by using verbal rehearsal on an expository passage), and the lowest was 17.1% (from using subject-generated loci on a descriptive passage).

The variability of these results emphasizes that it is no simple matter to rule when a specific mnemonic is the best tool for the job. In this particular study, verbal rehearsal was clearly better than the place method for written presentations of both descriptive and expository texts (regardless of whether the loci were generated by the experimenter or the subject). However, when the written text was narrative, both verbal rehearsal and the loci method (where the loci were supplied by the experimenter) achieved the same level (in fact the loci method was slightly superior, but not significantly). And when the text was presented orally (as it would be in a lecture or seminar), the loci method was clearly superior to verbal rehearsal for all types of text — with subject-generated loci always superior to experimenter-generated loci.

It does seem clear, however, that the best time to use the place method is in an oral situation — when you are either listening or speaking.

The place method is particularly useful:

When you are listening to a lecture.

When you are giving a speech.

For written text, when the text is expository rather than narrative or descriptive.

The pegword mnemonic

The pegword mnemonic is based on the same idea as the place method, but uses numbers rather than places as cues. These numbers are transformed into visual images by means of the following simple rhyme:

one is a bun

two is a shoe

three is a tree

four is a door

five is a hive

six is sticks

seven is heaven

eight is a gate

nine is a vine (also, variously: nine is wine; nine is a line)

ten is a hen

The rhyme must be learned by rote until it is over-learned. Accordingly, the pegword method is not as quickly mastered as the place method, where cues already over-learned are used.

It does however have an advantage over the place method, in that the items learned are not tied to a particular sequence, and therefore it's not necessary to recall the whole list to retrieve a single item. That is, you can simply ask yourself what number 7 is, without having to go through the first six items to get there.

It is also ideal for learning numbered lists, such as the cranial nerves:

1. is a bun and cranial nerve 1 is olfactory. So you could visualize a nose diving into a bun.

2. is a shoe, and cranial nerve 2 is optic: imagine a shoe with eyes.

3. is a tree, and cranial nerve 3 is oculomotor — so continuing with the eye theme, and bringing in something that cues us to motor, visualize a motorbike ridden by a Cyclops (a one-eyed giant) running into a tree.

4. is a door, and cranial nerve 4 is trochlear — still with the eyes, and bringing in a truck to cue us to the name: put an eye on a door and a truck careening into it.

5. is a hive, and cranial nerve 5 is trigeminal, which relates to the jaw — so something to cue the jaw and something to cue the name (three gems): imagine a skull with three gemstones wedged in its gaping jaw, sitting on top of a beehive.

6. is sticks, and cranial nerve 6 is abducens — back to the eyes, and bringing in a ufo to cue the name (alien abduction!): a flying saucer with a huge eye

painted on it is crashing on a pile of sticks.

7. is heaven, and cranial nerve 7 is facial, so a disembodied face among clouds, upon which an angel is resting.

8. is a gate, and cranial nerve 8 is auditory, so visualize a gate with ears.

9. is wine, and cranial nerve 9 is glossopharyngeal, which relates to the throat, so imagine a glossy photo of yourself pouring wine down your throat.

10. is a hen, and cranial nerve 10 is vagus, which relates to the heart: visualize a hen carrying a heart, all pale and fuzzy (vague) in its beak.

The rhyming pegwords I gave you only went to 10, but we can add to this traditional list:

11 is a lemon

12 is shelves

11. Cranial nerve 11 is accessory, which relates to head movement, so we put lemons and a shrunken head into a bag (accessory).

12. Cranial nerve 12 is hypoglossal, which relates to the tongue, so we use a hypodermic needle to cue the name, and imagine the tongue, sticking out from some shelves, being stuck with the needle.

To return to the principle I discussed under the keyword method: images are effective to the extent to which the elements interact actively and meaningfully. For this reason, I found my seventh image poor. There is no particular connection between the face and the angel in this image. A better image would be an angel having a facial, perhaps with lurid green sludge over their face.

The pegword method can be considerably extended using the coding mnemonic. We'll look at that in the discussion of that mnemonic.

APPLYING THE PEGWORD METHOD

One of the potential problems with the pegword method is the question of how many lists you can hang off the same pegs. However, one early study[1] found no problems with interference when volunteers learned six consecutive reorderings of the same nouns (although the lists did not have to be remembered very long, and I strongly suspect interference would increasingly have become a problem for memory over time).

Similarly, a recent study[2] found dramatic benefits from using a combined pegword-keyword mnemonic to remember three different lists (10 highest mountains, 10 tallest waterfalls, 10 largest volcanoes), as well as two training lists: tested five days after learning these, average recall was 64%, 51%, and 31% respectively for those using the mnemonic, compared to 42%, 26%, and 17% for those using their own methods. In other words, there is interference, but using the pegword mnemonic is decidedly better than not using it. Nor do we know how much more effective the mnemonic may have been if the lists had been spaced out.

Interference is always going to occur if you try and learn different lists at the same time, regardless of method. I feel the best way is to space out your lists, achieving a certain level of mastery of one list before tackling a new one. If you do feel you're likely to confuse the lists, you might find it helpful to provide a distinctive mark for each list (that appears in the mnemonic image for each item on the list).

Although concrete, visualizable words are always better if you can find appropriate ones, two studies[2] have found abstract pegwords (e.g., one is fun, two is true, ...) could be just as effective as concrete ones. But this has not been found consistently[4]. It seems to depend on your imagery ability[5].

The pegword method

- requires you to learn the pegs very very well

- enables you to go directly to any item on a list

- is the best method for a numbered list

The link method

Like the place method and the pegword method, the link method uses visual images to link items together. However, instead of using a well-learned structure to anchor the new information, items are linked to each other. In this way it is like the story method.

However, the link method requires less thematic coherence than the story method — you are essentially building a chain, in which the only requirement is that each item forms a visual image with the item next to it.

Thus, for our 12 cranial nerves, you could form the following images:

- a **nose** with the **eyes** above;

- the **eyes** on the handlebars, **riding a motorbike**;

- the **motorbike** hitting a **truck**;

- the **truck** spilling its load of **3 gems**;

- a **ufo** coming down, **abducting** the **truck**driver;

- an alien (**abductor**) ripping off the driver's **face**;

- the **ears** falling off the **face**;

- the **ears** falling onto a **glossy photo**;

- the **glossy photo** pinned to a **pink heart**;

- the **pink heart** being tucked into a bag (**accessory**);

- the bag (**accessory**) being pierced with a **hypodermic**.

EFFECTIVENESS OF THE LINK METHOD

There has been very little research into the effectiveness of the link method, but findings from two early studies[1] found dramatic benefits from using this method to learn lists of unrelated nouns after a single presentation.

Bugelski, for example, found the average recall of a 20-word list without using the method was around 10 words, of which only half were remembered in the correct order. In comparison, half as many more were remembered using the link method, and there was markedly better order recall. In the most effective condition, in which college students were given 6 seconds to study each word, an average of 15 words were recalled in correct sequence, with an average of 17 recalled overall — this compares to an average of 5.5 and 9.7 when the students were simply told to try and learn the words in the order given.

Nor did the students receive much instruction in the technique — they were simply told to form an image of each word in their mind and to try to incorporate this image with the prior image in some interaction. This suggests that this is a method easily mastered — although like all mnemonics, practice will certainly make you much more fluent at implementing it!

The study also showed that the method had a marked effect on persistence and consistency.

Those using their own methods showed the typical pattern of remembering the first and last items best, with a sudden drop after the 3rd item (the primacy and recency effects). By the 7th item, these students had essentially given up. Those using the link method, however, simply showed a slow decline, with no precipitous drop. By the 7th item, 85% of the link method group were still learning.

Perhaps most importantly, the study found wide individual variability: around a sixth of the link method group (16 out of 96 students) recalled all 20 items, in sequence, after a single presentation. Some of these could, when asked, return all 20 in the reverse order.

This emphasizes how the effectiveness of a strategy depends as much on the individual as on the strategy itself.

Advantages & disadvantages of the link method

- doesn't require a pre-learned structure

- is easily learned

- doesn't allow you to go directly to any item, but requires you to work your way through the chain until you get to the item

- requires visualization skill

Part IV
Advanced
mnemonics

Through this book, we have moved through the different mnemonic systems in terms of increasing difficulty. Having begun with the simplest, most familiar mnemonics, we moved to the keyword method, which is a powerful and effective technique in its own right, and also the component that turns the list-mnemonics into truly useful strategies. In this final section, we will look at another mnemonic that is both very powerful in its own right, and a component that greatly expands the possibilities of the list-mnemonics.

In the last chapter, I will bring all this information together, to help you use these mnemonics most effectively.

Coding mnemonics

A SYSTEM FOR REMEMBERING NUMBERS

Most people find numbers — phone numbers, personal identification numbers, dates, and so on — more difficult to remember than words. That is, of course, why businesses try to get phone numbers that correspond to some relevant word. The system whereby this is possible — the linking of certain letters to the different digits on a telephone calling pad — is a kind of coding mnemonic. Basically, coding mnemonics are systems that transform numbers into words.

Because words are much easier for most of us to remember, this is a good way to remember numbers, but it's not the only one. If you have a facility for numbers, or an existing store of memorized numbers (dates, baseball scores, running times, whatever), you can use those memorized numbers or your understanding of mathematical patterns to remember new numbers.

In one well-known experiment[1], for example, the subject was able (after 250 hours of practice!) to recall up to 82 digits after hearing them at the rate of one digit a second. This subject was a runner, and used his knowledge of record times to make the digit strings more memorable.

The difficulty with a coding system is that you can't use it effectively until you have fluently memorized the codes, to the extent that the linked letter (if encoding) or digit (if decoding) comes automatically to mind.

This requirement makes this sort of mnemonic the costliest of all the mnemonics — that is, it takes the most time and effort to master.

Of course, the pegword mnemonic is also a coding system, in a way — which is why it's harder to master than the method of loci. But the pegword mnemonic is easier than the digit-letter substitution mnemonic.

There are two reasons why:

- the pegs and their numbers are connected by simple rhymes;

- the construction of a composite image incorporating the peg and the item to be learned is less constrained than the finding of a suitable word constructed from the required letters.

Let me show you what I mean.

On the next page I have set out the best-known digit-letter code. It's important to note the system is based on sound rather than actual letters, so various similar-sounding letters are regarded as equivalent:

Now these substitutions weren't chosen arbitrarily. The

inventor has tried his best to make them easy to remember. But as you can see, some of the rationales are rather contrived. If you think you can come up with codes that are easier for you to remember, feel free to change them — just bear in mind the dangers of confusability. For example, you could code *f* for *5*, but there is a strong risk of becoming confused between *4* and *5* when decoding.

0 = s, z, soft c	(*zero* starts with a *s* sound)
1 = t, d, th	(there's *1* downstroke in *t*)
2 = n	(*2* downstrokes in *n*)
3 = m	(*3* downstrokes in *m*)
4 = r	(*r* is the last letter of *four*)
5 = l	(*l* is 50 in Roman numbers)
6 = sh, ch, j, soft g	(*six* has a sort of *sh* sound)
7 = k, q, hard g, hard c	(number *7* is embedded in *k*)
8 = f, v	(both *8* and *f* have two loops)
9 = p, b	(*9* is *p* the wrong way round)

Once you've encoded the digits into letters, you can turn numbers into words or phrases or rhymes. Only consonants are used for coding. This means you can throw vowels (and also, in this system, *w*, *h* and *y*) in as necessary.

In this way the date 1945 could be encoded as *tprl*, which could be turned into *top role, to pour low, tie a poor owl, tip or lie, top rail.* Or *dprl*: *die poorly! tbrl*: *tuba role*; *dbrl*: *dab rule.*

You see what I mean about constraints. However, there is enough give in the system to make it possible to always come up with *something.*

If you do want to learn this particular system, there is a mnemonic that may help you memorize the 0-9 codes (from Bower, 1978): **S**atan **m**ay **r**e**l**ish **c**off**ee p**ie. *Why* will help you remember which consonants can be used freely, like vowels.

The system also allows you to use doubled consonants where the sound doesn't change (which is mostly). For example, *dipper, dabble, squirrel.* Compare these to *accent,* where the first *c* is hard (7) and the second *c* is soft (0).

Similarly, a silent consonant doesn't count. Thus *knee* equates to 2 and not 72. Less obviously, words like *would, could, should* don't count the *l*. But I'm not sure I like this myself. I'm very aware of how words are spelled, and tend to 'see' words as I hear them. I think whether or not you count silent consonants depends on your awareness of what the words look like.

A similar issue of personal preference is whether you regard *ng* as a variant of hard *g* (7), or two sounds: *n* and *g* (27).

x generally makes the sound of *ks* (70), but when it starts a word (xylophone, xenon) it's often more a soft *z* sound (0).

You can see why this system takes more training than the other systems! And why this mnemonic is the least studied of the major mnemonics. In those few studies that have been done, there are usually only one or two subjects. This is not surprising when you consider the number of hours needed to achieve mastery of this system. These studies have invariably focused on training their subjects to memorize very long strings of digits quickly. It's hard to imagine the everyday circumstances in which this would be a useful skill for most of us.

Having said that, there are a number of occasions when you want to remember shorter numbers — say four, or seven, or even nine digits. And the code really isn't as hard to learn as it might seem, looking at it. A little practice coding numbers into letters, and back again, works wonders in cementing this in your brain.

One study[2] that did involve a number of students, and, most interesting of all, did compare the performance of students who learnt the mnemonic with the performance of students instructed in general cognitive strategies (such as chunking and clustering) but not mnemonics, found impressive results with the mnemonic. Over 45% of the mnemonic students recalled all 20 digits in a 4x5 matrix, compared to 7% of the cognitive students. Over 85% recalled at least 16 digits, compared to 35%. Even more impressively, 43% recalled all 50 digits from a 50-digit matrix (4x12+1x2), and 78% recalled at least 45. The comparison group in this case were general psychology students who had received no particular cognitive training — none remembered more than 34 digits. Indeed, only 3 of the 37 mnemonic students who learned the 50-digit matrix did as badly as any of the general students, and these 3 had all failed to learn the mnemonic properly.

The mnemonic students had spent four 75-minute classes studying the mnemonic, plus about an hour's practice outside class. They studied (but didn't memorize) a list of 100 keywords (for the numbers 0-99), but didn't have much practice memorizing matrices (one 60-second practice with a 20-digit matrix).

Keeping it simple

Remember the codes with: **Satan may relish coffee pie**

Vowels and consonants **why** don't count

Avoid **x**, **ng**, silent consonants.

Remember doubled consonants that sound like one only count as one

Remember it's the sound that matters.

EXTENDING THE CODING METHOD WITH OTHER MNEMONICS

The coding mnemonic on its own is simply a way of transforming poorly-remembered numbers into better-remembered words. But words and phrases, as we have seen, vary in their memorability. Studies[3] have shown that the difficulty of coming up with easily remembered words is sufficiently great that even with two-digit numbers, students don't easily come up with memorable words when time is limited. Thus, only when good words are supplied by the experimenter, does the method produce significantly better recall.

Of course, the key phrase here is *when time is limited.* In normal (non-experimental) circumstances, you will have as much time as you need to come up with good words and practice them sufficiently. But the limitation does point to the difficulty of the method for novices (it may well be, as Higbee suggests, that self-generated coded words are more effective when the mnemonist is more skilled).

It also points to the reason why lists of coded words are popular — however, those do require that you sit down and memorize them all! Whether or not that time and effort is worth it to you depends on how much you're going to use it. And that depends, in part, on *how* you are going to use it. I have talked of the coding mnemonic as a transformational strategy, but it is also a powerful tool as part of what Higbee calls a *mental filing system.*

But first, let's explore more deeply the use of the coding mnemonic in remembering numbers. Let's try the code out on some longer numbers.

237-812-469 = n-m-k-f-t-n-r-sh-p

Any meek feet now rush by.

Here's another:

3794-2106-6512-8843 = m-k-p-r-n-t-s-sh-sh-l-t-n-f-f-r-m

My keeper and Sasha shall wait in a fever home.

As you can see, the longer the numbers, the harder to make a memorable sentence! But I didn't cheat — no tweaking of the numbers (which I produced off the top of my head) in order to create a more meaningful sentence. On the other hand, you could probably come up with better sentences if you spent more time on it (I came up with these in just a few minutes).

Another way of dealing with long numbers is to break them into 2-digit groups and use a pre-learned list of 100 one- and two-digit words which you then convert into a series of linked images.

Thus 237-812-469 = 23-78-12-46-9 → gnome-coffee-tin-rash-pie

3794-2106-6512-8843 =3-79-42-10-66-51-28-84-3 → ham-cap-rain-toes-judge-wallet-knife-fire-ham

You'll notice that in the second example, even though the number would have broken evenly into pairs, I put a single digit at the beginning and the end (not ideal in this particular case since the number began and ended with the same digit). I did this because otherwise one of the pairs would have been 06. The other solution would have been to make a combined image (a witch (6) with a hose (0)).

If you prefer words to images, you could also make these words into a story rather than a chain of images. For example, the gnome pours his coffee into a tin, gets a rash, and solaces himself with a pie. Here you can see the importance of making sure your code-words are all nouns — that way you know that only the nouns in the story signify numbers.

There are other ways to organize long numbers. In the case of the runner who used track times, for example, the times provided small groups of digits, which the runner then organized into small clusters, and then into super-clusters.

Another strategy is to use the place method.

In one study[4], for example, a subject memorized 100 concrete nouns to match the numbers 0 to 99, and 40 Berlin landmarks (in a particular order). They could then encode a string of 80 digits by mentally attaching the image for each digit pair to the landmark.

But it did take many hours to master this!

In another study[5], a subject combined the story mnemonic with the place method by making a story for each group of 10 words (20 digits — again, it was first necessary to memorize 100 concrete nouns for each possible digit-pair combination), and then placing each story in a different setting. These settings were of course always used in the same order. Using this combination resulted in fewer errors and recall failures than the story mnemonic on its own. Of course, as always with studies involving coding mnemonics, we are drawing conclusions from the performance of one or two people only, so we cannot be too firm about this! However, it does make sense.

Practical uses for coding mnemonics

In the study situation, there is quite a lot of numerical information that you might need or be interested in learning. Historical dates; mathematical formulae; geographical facts.

Let's look at how we can combine three different mnemonics to remember the lengths of the ten longest rivers (in miles):

1.   Nile (4140 miles)

2. Amazon (3990 miles)

3. Yangtse (3960 miles)

4. Yenisei-Angara (3445 miles)

5. Ob-Irtysh (3360 miles)

6. Hwang Ho (3005 miles)

7. Zaire/Congo (2900 miles)

8. Amur (2800 miles)

9. Mekong (2795 miles)

10. Lena (2730 miles)

First, let's use the coding mnemonic to convert the lengths:

1. Nile 4140 = r-t-r-s = rotors, raiders, readers

2. Amazon 3990 = m-p-p-s = my pipes

3. Yangtse 3960 = m-p-sh-s = impish ass

4. Yenisei-Angara 3445 = m-r-r-f = more or few, more rev

5. Ob-Irtysh 3360 = m-m-sh-s = mommy shoes

6. Hwang Ho 3005 = m-s-s-f = mass shave, miss safe

7. Zaire/Congo 2900 = n-p-s-s = any passes

8. Amur 2800 = n-f-s-s = no fusses

9.   Mekong 2795 = n-k-p-f = neck puff

10. Lena 2730 = n-k-m-s = hen games

They're not brilliant, I know. Sometimes numbers will fall nicely into meaningful words, but more often they won't. Still, you'll be surprised how much these weird phrases help.

Now we need to use the keyword mnemonic to turn the names of the rivers into something concrete and familiar.

Nile — nail

Yangtse — ant sea (a sea of ants)

Yenisei-Angara — nice anchor (*nice* is not concrete, but you can attach it by always thinking *nice anchor* when visualizing it)

Ob-Irtysh — (observe the) yurt

Hwang Ho — hanging (image of a noose hanging from a gallows)

Zaire/Congo — stair (not using Congo because of its similarity to Mekong)

Amur — a mule

Mekong — King Kong

Lena — lion

You'll notice I didn't give a keyword for Amazon; I felt the female Amazon would provide an adequate image.

Now we can use the pegword mnemonic to provide our ordered list. So we tie our keywords to the pegwords to produce the following images:

1. a nail in a bun

2. an Amazon with one big shoe

3. a sea of ants around a tree

4. an anchored door

5. someone watching a yurt with a beehive hanging from its pole

6. an axe among sticks next to the gallows

7. stairway to heaven

8. a mule nudging a gate

9. King Kong drinking wine

10. a lion ripping apart a hen

Once you've worked on visualizing these images and got them well down, you can then connect the images to your sentences. Don't worry if your images aren't as clear as you think they should be; I rely equally on the words as much as the images — but it helps to visualize as much as you can while thinking on the words.

Now you've got these word-images (and it really does take very little practice), you can stick the coded phrases on.

1. a nail in a bun: **rotors** (helicopter blades) trying to lift the nailed bun

2. an Amazon with one big shoe: tripping over her big shoe, she drops her blowpipes: **My pipes**! she cries

3. a sea of ants around a tree: an **impish ass** (donkey) grins as he flicks ants at the tree

4. an anchored door: the door strains to move against its anchor; I shout: **More rev**!

5. someone watching a yurt with a beehive hanging from its pole: the observer is wearing **mommy shoes**

6. an axe among sticks next to the gallows: a mass of people lining up to be shaved by the axe (**mass shave**)

7. stairway to heaven: "**any passes**?" I ask anxiously

8. a mule nudging a gate: going through easily; "**no fusses**"

9. King Kong drinking wine: big **neck puff** around his neck

10. a lion ripping apart a hen: **hen games**!

It all sounds very strained and unnecessarily complicated if you simply read all this! You absolutely cannot appreciate this method until you try it. It really is much simpler than it appears (although still not a simple strategy). However, it is vital that you build up the strategy step by step. In this case, for example, you must be fully confident of the standard 1-10 pegwords (1 is a bun, etc) first; then you fix the rivers to the pegwords firmly; and finally you attach the coded phrases.

Notice also how my choice of phrases was modified by the pegword-river images. For example, originally I preferred 'raiders', but when I came to attach it to the nailed bun, I found it easier to integrate helicopter blades. Similarly, 'more or few' made more sense to me until I considered it in relation to the anchored door, when 'more rev' fit in better.

Again, if you actually do this exercise and try to learn these images, you'll see for yourself how the easiest ones to learn are the ones that make more meaningful, more tightly integrated, word-pictures.

I remarked earlier on the awkwardness of some of these phrases. There is another way of dealing with the codes — you can make a sentence with each word in the sentence starting with the letter you want to remember. Thus:

Rust **d**own **r**oof **s**lates.

Many **p**irates **p**ester **s**almon.

Monkeys **p**ick **sh**ells **s**lowly.

Men **r**ead **r**ed **f**ables.

Monks **m**ine **sh**ell **s**ands.

May **s**ell **s**uper **f**eet.

None **p**ay **s**illy **s**ums.

Names **f**or **s**imple **s**ongs.

Never **k**ick **p**oor **f**ellows.

Nearly **k**isses **m**y **s**on.

There are two ways you could attach these to the rivers. You could do it in a similar way to the coded phrases: as you visualize your nail in a bun, you say *Read the right song*; as you picture your Amazon in her big shoe, you think: *Many pirates pester salmon*; and so on.

(By the way, never get so hung up on specific mnemonics you forget to use other information. It does help if you pay attention to features such as, in this case, that only the first sentence starts with a different letter, an R, while the next five begin with M and the last four with N. In the same way, with the cranial nerves, it helps to note that there are three Os, two Ts and three As; that four of the nerves are to do with the eyes and two have *gloss* in the name. These can all be useful cues that will help trigger the mnemonic if you forget it.)

The other method of attaching the coded sentences to the river names is to keep the two mnemonics as completely separate lists, and incorporate the river keyword into the sentence:

(Nails) Rust through roof slates.

(With the Amazon) Many pirates pester salmon.

(In the ant sea) Monkeys pick shells slowly.

(At anchor) Men read red fables.

(In the yurt, observant) Monks mine shell sands.

(Hanged Whores) May sell super feet.

(On the stairs) None pay silly sums.

(Mule) Names for simple songs.

(King Kong) Never kicks poor fellows.

(A lion) Nearly kisses my son.

In this instance I think the coded phrases, however awkward they may sound, work better than these mnemonic sentences, but there are circumstances in which you may well find a sentence works better.

All of this sounds terribly complicated, I know. But the point is not that these mnemonics are simple — they aren't! Nor does the use of mnemonics mean you don't need to put in any effort; it's not a magic trick (or perhaps that is exactly what it is — magic tricks look very impressive to the audience, but the magician has had to practice hard to produce them).

The point of these mnemonics is to make raw facts such as these (facts which are not meaningfully connected) more memorable. And they do, although you probably won't believe it until you try it. But although the method I've described may seem very complicated, it really does make learning and remembering these facts much easier than the alternative: brute force (rote repetition).

Dealing with decimals

Higbee suggests[2] that you can use *s* to mark decimals. Because numbers will never start with 0, coded words will never begin with *s* (of course they may begin with *sh*). Thus you are free to use *s* as an initial to indicate a decimal point. For example:

389.75 = m-f-p s-k-l = move by skill (note the *s* must start the word on the other side of the decimal point; you can't just put it into a word, for otherwise it would indicate a 0)

3.14159 = m s-t-r-l-p = my stroll-by

0.469 = s-r-sh-p = sir sheep (note you don't need to encode the marker 0 before the decimal point)

Of course, if you do use this, it means you should never start a word with *s* when you are transforming a long number into several words, unless it is a decimal point.

Another way of doing it is to replace a decimal point with a comma in your phrase or sentence, but this works better if you're seeing the word as well as hearing it.

RETRIEVAL

One of the reasons why coding mnemonics are more effortful is that it takes practice before you can automatically and fluently code numbers into letters. The other reason is that it takes an equal amount of practice to *decode* automatically and fluently! In other words, it is not enough to practice turning numbers into words. To master this strategy, you need to also practice turning words into numbers.

I suggest that if you want to master this technique, you practice transforming odd phrases and sentences as you read the newspaper, or other casual material (like the back of the cereal box).

OTHER LANGUAGES MAY WORK BETTER!

While I have restricted my discussion to English, it shouldn't go unremarked that the coding mnemonic may be easier in some other languages. Japanese, for example, is a syllabic language, meaning they have a different sign for each consonant-vowel pair. Moreover, because they have built their written language on top of the characters imported from China, their digits are each associated with two or more different pronunciations. For these reasons, transforming numbers into letter-sounds is sufficiently easy and obvious that many Japanese spontaneously use such a mnemonic[6].

USING CODING TO EXTEND THE PEGWORD MNEMONIC

As mentioned, the value of this code goes beyond simply creating words or phrases that help you remember numbers. You can also use it to create concrete images that can become pegs.

Let's look at possible words for various numbers:

1: **t**ie (man's necktie)

2: ho**n**ey (remember, h and y don't count!)

3: ha**m**

4: ea**r**

5: ow**l**

6: wi**tch**

7: ya**k**; e**gg;**

8: **f**ae; i**vy**

9: **p**ie

10: **t**oe**s**

11: **t**oa**d**; **d**eath

12: **tin**

13: **t**i**m**e; **d**i**m**e

14: **d**ee**r**

15: **t**owe**l**

16: **d**i**sh**

17: **d**u**ck**

18: **d**ove

19: **t**o**p**; **t**a**p**

20: **n**o**s**e

And so on, up to 99.

As you can readily appreciate, this enables you to greatly extend the pegword method. Moreover, although finding concrete words becomes increasingly hard as the number of digits increases, you can use a kind of hierarchical organization to extend your pegwords without having to come up with appropriate words. For example, by tying colors or other adjectives to particular groups, so that the nouns for numbers 100-199 are all described by one particular adjective, those for 200-299 by another.

The use of pegwords in this way is clearly not aimed only at numbered lists (although it can be very useful if you want to memorize Bible verses). It is in fact the basis for a mental filing system that you can use to organize huge amounts of information, to make for easy retrieval.

However, there is no research or even anecdotal evidence of successful use of such large systems, and I believe it is only likely to be of any use for experts — those who are not only expert in mnemonics, but also in other, meaning-based, memory strategies. So I do not recommend you dive into this particular system, but concentrate first on building your expertise in all the other (simpler!) strategies that help you learn and remember.

The coding mnemonic

- requires the most time to master

- is an effective means of remembering numbers

- can be combined with the list-mnemonics to learn very long numbers

- can be combined with the pegword method to extend the number of pegs

---

Mastering mnemonics

WHAT MNEMONICS ARE GOOD FOR

Before we discuss choosing the right mnemonic strategy, let's talk about when mnemonics are the best choice.

Assessing the text and the task

As I discuss in my book *Effective notetaking*, the first step in choosing the right strategy for a task is to accurately analyze the problem — indeed, to identify that there *is* a problem. One of the main reasons poor learners are less successful is because they are often unaware that they haven't understood something, or that they won't remember something without deliberate effort.

So, your first task is to recognize when you need to make a deliberate effort. Then you need to accurately define the problem so that you know which of all the tools you (should) have in your toolbox is the right one for the task.

Defining the problem involves three actions:

- articulating your goal

- defining the retrieval context

- evaluating the material

I cannot emphasize enough that the first step in any memory task is to clearly specify your goal — at all levels, because goals are nested.

For example, you may have the overall goal of getting a degree, the more specific goal of passing a particular exam, and the still more specific goal of understanding a particular chapter, or of committing to memory certain facts. You may have the ultimate goal of getting a good job, and so aim to be one of the top graduates of your year, requiring you to get top marks in this specific subject, and thus you need to learn more than a student who only aims to pass.

To accurately define these more specific goals, it helps to understand the wider goals they're nested in. To learn the 'right' material — the material you need to learn to fulfill these goals — you need to have these goals clearly articulated.

Part of articulating that goal is realizing the circumstances in which you are going to be retrieving the material. For example, do you need it for an exam? for multi-choice questions or essay answers? for a classroom discussion? for an oral presentation? to build expertise?

Different situations make different demands on you. You may need to:

- **select** the relevant information;

- **organize** the relevant information into a clear structure;

- **understand** the information;

- **recognize** the correct information;

- **respond** with the right information when given a cue;

- **retrieve** the right information when needed.

My book *Effective notetaking* discusses in great detail the first three tasks (selection, organization, comprehension) — all of which, if done with sufficient attention, should be sufficient for recognition and may well be sufficient for recall. Mnemonics of course is only about recall — retrieving information in response to some cue or when needed.

So, given that you've identified the need for retrieval, how do you know if you need mnemonics?

There are two parts to this answer. The first depends on the information itself, on the degree to which it connects with other information you know well, and whether or not it needs to be remembered in essence or with precision (a particular order; specific words). The second depends on you and the retrieval context, on how likely you are to be able to retrieve the information in the situation you will be in.

If you suffer from memory blocks when anxious or stressed, for example, mnemonics are a very good way of providing an additional access point to the information. (A side note on this problem: recent research found that those who suffer badly from test anxiety were considerably helped by spending ten minutes before the exam writing out their worries. This is thought to help free up valuable working memory space that's being cluttered with these anxieties.)

The bottom line is:

Mnemonics are the best type of strategy for cueing well-learned information (for overcoming memory blocks or for reminding you of the order of information or the names of things).

Mnemonics are the best strategy for memorizing arbitrary details.

Mnemonics can provide a retrieval structure (a framework to help you remember) when you lack the expertise to use comprehension strategies such as elaborative interrogation or self-explanation.

CHOOSING THE RIGHT STRATEGY FOR THE TASK

Given that you've decided that the situation calls for a mnemonic strategy, how do you decide which one is the best? There are three main factors you should consider:

- Information attributes

- Retrieval requirements

- Personal characteristics

Let's look at information attributes first.

As I've said, mnemonics are primarily for meaningless (which means unconnected) information. However, meaningfulness is not an either/or attribute. It is a product of the interaction between the individual and the

126

information, and it varies across individuals, across time (what is meaningless for you at the beginning of your studies will hopefully not be meaningless for you by the end of them!), and across context.

Moreover, there are different types of meaningfulness. While deep meaning, and understanding, comes from connection to your existing knowledge, a certain level of meaning comes simply from internal relatedness — connection between the bits of information being presented to you.

Different degrees of this internal relatedness lend themselves to different mnemonic strategies. Thus at one end of the scale, rhythm and rhyme require a relatively high degree of relatedness, while at the other end, the place method requires no relatedness at all.

In general, the easiest and most common mnemonic strategies are also the ones that require a reasonable degree of relatedness:

- First-letter mnemonics

- Rhythm, rhyme, and song

- Story method

Although as a general rule the imagery-based list-mnemonics don't require much internal relatedness, the three different imagery list-learning strategies do vary in terms of the relatedness they require between the list items. Some items, for example, are linked by being sequential (ordered by number) — these obviously lend themselves to the pegword method. Others will be linked by being consequential (connected by cause and effect) — these lend themselves to the link method. Some items (particularly in experimental studies) may be arbitrarily related — this is the case where the place method is likely to be the best choice.

You'll recall also that the place method is particularly recommended in oral situations (such as when listening to lectures). Directly encoding information into a mnemonic while listening to a lecture is of course a job for a skilled practitioner! However, it certainly has its advantages if you do get sufficiently skilled, and in such cases a visual mnemonic seems to be better than a verbal one.

This idea that visual mnemonics are better for situations where you hear the information, and verbal mnemonics for situations where you see the information (as in written text) is a useful guideline, but comes with plenty of addendums.

For example, there's some evidence[1] that using the pegword method is less disrupted than the place method by doing another visual task at the same time, because while it is visual, it is not *spatial*, as the place method is (which thus puts more demands on your visuospatial pathway).

It's also speculated[2] that in the case of written texts we need to consider the content. Descriptions of visual scenes should be regarded as visuospatial; narratives as causal or thematic sequences of events in time; expository texts as following some logical process. If this is so, it may be that the place method is best used on expository texts, the link method on narratives, and the pegword method on static visual descriptions.

In a similar vein, it has been suggested that the story method is better for abstract items, and imagery methods for concrete items. This presupposes that you're not using the keyword method to transform an abstract or difficult word into something more concrete and memorable, or that the best transformations are in fact abstract words.

Remember that list-mnemonics are not restricted to actual lists, but are useful for any ordered information.

In the case of numbered lists, of course, the pegword method (possibly in conjunction with the coding mnemonic) is the best tool. But again, you should think of 'numbered' in broad terms: if you want to be able to go directly to any item on the list, and not be constrained by having to work through it item-by-item, you are better with a numbered list.

A major drawback of the place and link methods is that, if you want a specific item, you must start from the beginning of the list and work your way through it until you reach the item. This reinforces the matching of these methods to information that is sequential or consequential.

Both the place and the pegword methods share the property that they require a pre-learned structure. This property has the advantage of providing a retrieval structure, but also the disadvantage that — because the structure is being re-used — the most recent list is the one most easily recalled and earlier lists are recalled with more difficulty[3].

You can reduce interference by giving each list its own special tag, or by using different places and pegwords. However, as with the keyword method, these techniques are best regarded as ways to enable you to quickly learn difficult items, which can then be consolidated with retrieval practice.

A list summarizing the tasks for which each mnemonic is most effective appears at the end of this chapter.

But don't forget the general principle: First and foremost, the purpose of mnemonics is to provide you with retrieval cues. Different mnemonics do that in different ways, but how effective they are depends not on the specific strategy but on how well that retrieval cue calls forth the information you need to know. That is the measure of your success, and it is according to that goal that you should determine which particular mnemonic will serve your purpose in any specific situation. So you always need to think about the circumstances in which you will be trying to retrieve the information.

CHOOSING THE STRATEGIES THAT ARE RIGHT FOR YOU

Finally, of course, these guidelines need to be considered in relation to your own abilities. It's been noted[4] that people with extraordinary memories show no uniformity in the strategies they use. In other words, there is no 'magic bullet', no single path to expertise. Some do it through their powerful imagery ability, some through their painfully mastered mnemonic expertise, others through their mastery of organizational strategies. The recipes are all different, and this underscores the fact that there are many effective memory strategies.

It's also been suggested[5] that this variety of techniques reflects the fact that all these highly skilled memorists have developed their skills on their own. This emphasizes the personal component — the importance of tailoring effective strategies to your own strengths and weaknesses, and with an eye to what you enjoy and find motivating.

SUCCESSFUL STRATEGIES NEED PRACTICE

No matter what strategy you use to remember something, you're going to need a certain amount of repetition to fix it in your brain. Mnemonics allow you to shortcut the process — the measure of how 'good' a particular mnemonic is, is indeed the degree to which it reduces the need for repetition. But no mnemonic is going to do away with the need for some repetition.

But repetition is not as straightforward a strategy as it might appear. We all know how to repeat something, but a lot of that repetition is wasted effort. The basic principle of effective repetition is quite simple: **effective repetition occurs at increasingly spaced intervals**.

How far apart should they be? Well, you should start by testing your memory after a very brief interval — perhaps an hour. If you're successful with that and the memory is fluent (easily recalled), you could leave the next test until bedtime — I say that not because of the time factor, but because sleep consolidates what you've learned that day, and I'm a big believer in refreshing your mind with that information just before sleep. If all goes well, you could leave it for 2 or 3 days, and then for a week.

How far you extend that depends on how long you need to remember the information for. If you want to remember it permanently, you should review it after two months, and probably again after six months. That's based on a recent large study[6] that explored the optimal gap between study and test: to remember for a week, the optimal gap was one day; for a month, it was 11 days, for 2 months (70 days) it was 3 weeks, and similarly for remembering for a year.

That's just to give you some idea — it really does depend on the individual, so don't take it as gospel! Moreover, it only looked at a very simplified learning situation and a single review.

The important principle is that you aim to find the maximum interval at which you can reliably recall the item. So if your memory fails, shorten the interval; if you succeed but with difficulty, keep the same interval; if you succeed easily, lengthen it. BUT: don't be fooled by early fluency into giving up your repetitions! The biggest reason for memory failure is people believing that being able to recall something easily means that they've learned it. Fluent recall is certainly a good signal if it happens after a lengthy period, say six months, but not if it happens within hours or a few days.

Of course, if the material you're trying to learn is something that 'naturally' comes up again and again (as most basic information will in the course of learning a subject), then you don't need to worry about this so much.

The other point that needs emphasizing is that by practice I mean *retrieval practice*, not simple rehearsal. In other words, you need to practice recalling the information, not just repeating it. The big advantage of mnemonics is that it gives you the help you need in the early stages to enable you to practice retrieval. It also reduces the need for quite so much retrieval practice. But never forget that retrieval practice is the most important part of learning.

And don't forget the importance of matching your retrieval practice to the retrieval contexts you expect! If you're going to need the know the capital given the country, you want to practice retrieving the capital from the country; if you're going to need to remember the second line of a verse after saying the first line, then you want to practice retrieving the second line keyword/image in response to the first line keyword/image.

The final point about practice that I want to make concerns its distribution. Distributing your practice doesn't simply involve spacing it out. It also involves interleaving it with other practice.

A study[7] that disentangled interleaving and spacing found that, when spacing was held constant, interleaving more than **doubled** test scores (77% vs 38%). This suggests that practicing different things is an effective way of improving your learning when time is limited.

It's also worth noting that the improved test scores from interleaving occurred despite the fact that performance was in fact poorer during practice. This brings us back to the perils of quick and easy fluency, and the notion of *desirable difficulty* (difficulties that the student can handle successfully, that engages processes that support learning[8]).

Principles of effective practice

Practice **retrieval**.

Space your practice at **increasing intervals**: aim for the time when you are just able to remember.

Interleave your practice with other topics.

A Final word

Never forget that being a successful student is far more about being a **smart user** of **effective strategies** than about being 'smart'. More important than intelligence, more important than the number of hours you put in, the most important ingredient in your success is knowing good strategies and knowing when and when not to use them. Mnemonics are just one type of learning strategy that you should have in your toolbox, and although they can be dramatically effective, they can't be the only skill you have. In particular, the effective use of mnemonics requires good selection skills — learning will only take you so far if you don't know what information you should be learning!

So, remember to clearly state your goals. Don't neglect developing your selection and notetaking skills. Never lose sight of the fact that successful learning is all about being able to retrieve the right information when it's needed, so think about the retrieval context when you're learning. Remember that even the best mnemonics require effective practice.

And if your confidence wavers, recite the mantra:

It's about knowing how, knowing when.

You know how and when. Now go and practice.

SUMMARY OF MNEMONIC STRATEGIES

Mnemonic	Tasks where it is most effective
Acronym	When the information is well-known to you, AND The order is important, AND The initial letters fall into a word or pseudo-word
Acrostic	When the information is well-known to you, AND The order is important
Rhythm & rhyme	When you have small amounts of information that can be expressed in simple terms
Keyword	When you need to remember words or terms that have no obvious connection with words you already know, OR When you need to remember pairs of associated items that have no meaningful connection (eg, capitals of states)
Face-name variant	When you wish to remember names and their associated images (such as artists' paintings, or types of animal)

Story	Especially for written text involving abstract terms, where items are linked sequentially or consequentially
Link	Especially for information heard, where items are concrete and linked sequentially or consequentially (as in narrative)
Loci	Especially for information heard, where items are concrete and the text is expository
Pegword	Especially when you have a numbered list, OR Where items are concrete and the text is descriptive, OR When you have many items and need to be able to go directly to any item on the list
Coding	When you need to remember numbers, OR You need to extend a numbered list

References

Mnemonics

Numbered citations:

1. Soler, M.J. & Ruiz, J.C. 1996. The spontaneous use of memory aids at different educational levels. *Applied Cognitive Psychology, 10*, 41-51.

2. Xu Cui, Jeter, C.B., Yang, D., Montague, P.R. & Eagleman, D.M. 2007. Vividness of mental imagery: Individual variability can be measured objectively. Vision Research, 47, 474-8.

Other references:

Bellezza, F.S. 1981. Mnemonic Devices: Classification, Characteristics, and Criteria. Review of Educational Research, 51 (2), 247-275.

Bellezza, F.S. 1983. Mnemonic-device instruction with adults. In Pressley, M. & Levin, J.R. (eds.) Cognitive strategy research: Psychological foundations. New York: Springer-Verlag.

Bower, G.H. 1972. Mental imagery and associative learning. In L.W. Gregg (ed.) Cognition in learning and memory. New York: Wiley.

Higbee, K.L. 1997. Novices, Apprentices, and

Mnemonists: Acquiring Expertise with the Phonetic Mnemonic. *Applied Cognitive Psychology, 11*, 147-161.

Morris, P.E. 1978. Sense and nonsense in traditional mnemonics. In M.M. Gruneberg, P.E. Morris & R.N. Sykes (eds.) Practical aspects of memory. London: Academic Press.

First-letter mnemonics

Numbered citations:

1. Boltwood, C.E. & Blick, K.A. 1970. The delineation and application of three mnemonic techniques. Psychonomic Science, 20, 339-341.

2. Nelson, D.L. & Archer, C.S. 1972. The first letter mnemonic. Journal of Educational Psychology, 63(5), 482-486.

3. Morris, P.E. & Cook, N. 1978. When do first letter mnemonics aid recall? British Journal of Educational Psychology, 48, 22-28.

4. Sergeant, A. & Gruneberg, M. 1997. The effectiveness of the first letter retrieval strategy in episodic memory. SARMAC II: Toronto, July 1997

5. Haring, M.J. & Fry, M.A. 1980. Facilitating prose recall with externally-produced mnemonics. Journal of Instructional Psychology, 7, 147-152.

Other references:

Carlson, L., Zimmer, J.W. & Glover, J.A. 1981. First-letter

mnemonics: DAM (Don't Aid Memory). *The Journal of General Psychology, 104*, 287-292.

Waite, C.J., Blick, K.A. & Boltwood, C.E. 1971. Prior use of the first letter technique. Psychological Reports, 29, 630.

Rhythm & Rhyme

Numbered citations:

1. Schmuckler, M.A. 1997. Expectancy Effects in Memory for Melodies. *Canadian Journal of Experimental Psychology, 51(4)*, 292-306.

2. Rainey, D.W. & Larsen, J.D. 2002. The Effect of Familiar Melodies on Initial Learning and Long-term Memory for Unconnected Text. *Music Perception, 20 (2)*, 173-186.

3. Kimmel, K.J. 1998. The Development and Evaluation of a Music Mnemonic-Enhanced Multimedia Computer-Aided Science Instructional Module. Dissertation submitted to the Faculty of the Virginia Polytechnic Institute and State University in partial fulfillment of the requirements for the degree of Doctor of Philosophy in Teaching and Learning. Available online at http://tinyurl.com/4qzxc

4. Cysarz, D., Von Bonin, D., Lackner, H., Moser, M. & Bettermann, H. 2004. Oscillations of heart rate and respiration synchronize during poetry recitation. *American Journal of Physiology - Heart and Circulatory Physiology, 287(2)*, H579-H587. http://www.rhythmen.de/downloads/ats_sync.pdf

5. Bernardi, L., Sleight, P., Bandinelli, G., Cencetti, S., Fattorini, L., Wdowczyc-Szulc, J. & Lagi, A. 2001. Effect of rosary prayer and yoga mantras on autonomic cardiovascular rhythms: comparative study. *BMJ, 323*, 1446-1449.

Other references:

Wallace, W. T. (1994). Memory for music: Effect of melody on recall of text. Journal of Experimental Psychology: Learning, Memory, & Cognition, 20, 1471-1485.

Yalch, R. F. (1991). Memory in a jingle jungle: Music as a mnemonic device in communicating advertising slogans. Journal of Applied Psychology, 76, 268-275.

Keyword method

Numbered citations:

1. Hall, J.W., Wilson, K.P. & Patterson, R.J. 1981. Mnemotechnics: Some limitations of the mnemonic keyword method for the study of foreign language vocabulary. Journal of Educational Psychology, 73, 345-57.

2. Rodríguez, M. & Sadoski, M. 2000. Effects of Rote, Context, Keyword, and Context/Keyword Methods on Retention of Vocabulary in EFL Classrooms. Language Learning, 50 (2), 385–412.
   Brown, T.S. & Perry, F.L. Jr. 1991. A Comparison of Three Learning Strategies for ESL Vocabulary Acquisition. TESOL Quarterly, 25 (4), 655-670.

3. Andreoff, G.R. & Yarmey, A.D. 1976. Bizarre imagery

and associative learning: A confirmation. Perceptual and Motor Skills, 43, 143-148.

Bergfeld, V.A., Choate, L.S. & Kroll, N.E. 1982. The effect of bizarre imagery on memory as a function of delay: Reconfirmation of the interaction effect. Journal of Mental Imagery, 6, 141-158.

Kroll, N.E.A., Schepeler, E.M. & Angin, K.T. 1986. Bizarre imagery: The misremembered mnemonic. Journal of Experimental Psychology: Learning, Memory and Cognition, 12, 42-53.

O'Brien, E.J. & Wolford, C.L.R. 1982. Effect of delay in testing on retention of plausible versus bizarre mental images. Journal of Experimental Psychology: Learning, Memory and Cognition, 8, 148-152.

Riefer, D.M. & Rouder, J.N. 1992. A multinomial modeling analysis of the mnemonic benefits of bizarre imagery. Memory & Cognition, 20, 601-611.

Webber, S.M. & Marshall, P.H. 1978. Bizarreness effects in imagery as a function of processing level and delay. Journal of Mental Imagery, 2, 291-300.

Campos, A., Amor, A. & González, M.A. 2002. Presentation of keywords by means of interactive drawings. The Spanish Journal of Psychology, 5(2), 102-109.

Campos, A. & Pérez, M.J. 1997. Mnemonic images and associated pair recall. Journal of Mental Imagery, 21, 73-82.

Kroll, N.E.A., Jaeger, G. & Dornfest, R. 1992. Metamemory for the bizarre. Journal of Mental Imagery, 16, 173-190.

Pra Baldi, A., De Beni, R., Cornoldi, C. & Cavedon, A. 1985. Some conditions for the occurrence of the bizarreness effect in free recall. British Journal of Psychology, 76, 427-436.

Riefer, D.M. & & LeMay, M.L. 1998. Memory for common and bizarre stimuli: A storage-retrieval analysis. Psychonomic Bulletin & Review, 5, 312-317.

Wollen, K.A. & Cox, S.D. 1981a. The bizarreness effect in a multitrial intentional learning task. Bulletin of the Psychonomic Society, 18, 296-298.

Wollen, K.A. & Cox, S.D. 1981b. Sentence cuing and the effectiveness of bizarre imagery. Journal of Experimental Psychology: Human Learning and Memory, 7, 386-392.

Marchal, A. & Nicolas, S. 2000. Is the picture-bizarreness effect a generation effect? Psychological Reports, 87, 331-340.

McDaniel, M.A., DeLosh, E.L. & Merritt, P.S. 2000. Order information and retrieval distinctiveness: Recall of common versus bizarre material. Journal of Experimental Psychology: Learning, Memory and Cognition, 26, 1045-1056.

Tess, D.E., Hutchinson, R.L., Treloar, J.H. & Jenkins, C.M. 1999. Bizarre imagery and distinctiveness: Implications for the classroom. Journal of Mental Imagery, 23, 153-170.

4. Beaton, A. A ., Gruneberg, M. M., Hyde, C. Shufflebottom, A. & Sykes, R.N. (2005). Facilitation of receptive and productive foreign vocabulary acquisition using the keyword method: The role of image quality. Memory, 13, 458-471.

5. Raugh, M.R., Schupbach, R.D. & Atkinson, R.C. 1977. Teaching a large Russian language vocabulary by the mnemonic keyword method. U.S. Office of Naval Research, Technical Report 256. http://suppes-corpus.stanford.edu/techreports/IMSSS_256.pdf

6. Raugh, M.R. & Atkinson, R.C. 1975. A mnemonic method for learning a second-language vocabulary. Journal of Educational Psychology, 67, l-16.

7. Wang, A.Y. & Thomas, M.H. 1992. The Effect of Imagery-Based Mnemonics on the Long-Term Retention of Chinese Characters. Language Learning, 42 (3), 359-376.
   Wang, A.Y. et al. 1989. Do Mnemonic Devices Lessen Forgetting? Paper presented at the Annual Meeting of the American Psychological Association (97th, New Orleans, LA, August 11-15, 1989).
   Wang, A.Y. et al. 1992. Keyword Mnemonic and Retention of Second-Language Vocabulary Words. Journal of Educational Psychology, 84, 520-8.
   Wang, A.Y. & Thomas, M.H. 1995. Effect of keywords on long-term retention: help or hindrance? Journal of Educational Psychology, 87, 468-75.
   Gruneberg, M.M.1998. A commentary on criticism of the keyword method of learning foreign languages. Applied Cognitive Psychology, 12, 529-532.
   Wang, A.Y. & Thomas, M.H. 1999. In defence of keyword experiments: a reply to Gruneberg's commentary. Applied Cognitive Psychology, 13, 283-287.

8. For example:
   Hall, J.W., Wilson, K.P. & Patterson, R.J. 1981. Mnemotechnics: Some limitations of the mnemonic keyword method for the study of foreign language vocabulary. Journal of Educational Psychology, 73, 345-357.
   King-Sears, M.E., Mercer, C.D. & Sindelar, P.T. 1992. Toward independence with keyword mnemonics: A strategy for science vocabulary instruction. Remedial and Special Education, 13, 22-333

9. Pressley, M., Levin, J.R., Digdon, N., Bryant, S.L. & Ray, K. 1983. Does method of item presentation affect keyword method effectiveness? Journal of Educational Psychology, 75, 686-91.

143

10.   Johnson, R.E. 1974. Abstractive processes in the remembering of prose. Journal of Educational Psychology, 66, 772-9.

Jones, M.S., Levin, M.E., Levin, J.R. & Beitzel, B.D. 2000. Can vocabulary-learning strategies and pair-learning formats be profitably combined? Journal of Educational Psychology, 92, 256-62.

McDaniel, M.A. & Pressley, M. 1984. Putting the keyword method in context. Journal of Educational Psychology, 76, 598-609.

McDaniel, M.A., Pressley, M. & Dunay, P.K. 1987. Long-term retention of vocabulary after keyword and context learning. Journal of Educational Psychology, 79, 87-9.

Pressley, M., Levin, J. & Miller, G. 1982. The keyword method compared to alternative vocabulary-learning strategies. Contemporary Educational Psychology, 7, 213-26.

Shing, Y.S. & Heyworth, R.M. 1992. Teaching English Vocabulary to Cantonese-speaking Students with the Keyword Method. Education Journal, 20, 113-129.

11.   Desrochers, A., Gélinas & Wieland, L.D. 1989. An application of the mnemonic keyword method to the acquisition of German nouns and their grammatical gender. Journal of Educational Psychology, 81, 25-32.

12. Chongde, L., Tsingan, L. & Hongyu, L. 2004. The effect of mnemonic key-letters method on Chinese children at risk in English vocabulary learning. Acta Psychologica Sinica, 36 (4), 482-490.

Other references:

Atkinson, R.C. 1975. Mnemotechnics in second-language learning. American Psychologist, 821-8.

Atkinson, R.C. & Raugh, M.R. 1975. An application of the mnemonic keyword method to the acquisition of a Russian vocabulary. Journal of Experimental Psychology: Human Learning and Memory, 104, 126-133.

Bird, S.A. & Jacobs, G.M. 1999. An Examination of the Keyword Method: How Effective Is It for Native Speakers of Chinese Learning English? *Asian Journal of English Language Teaching, 9*, 75-97.

Campos, A., Amor, A. & González, M.A. 2004. The importance of the keyword-generation method in keyword mnemonics. Experimental Psychology, 51(2), 1-7.

Campos, A., González, M.A. & Amor, A. 2003. Limitations of the mnemonic-keyword method. Journal of General Psychology, 130(4), 399-413.

Carney, R.N. & Levin, J.R.1994. Combining Mnemonic Strategies to Remember Who Painted What When. Contemporary Educational Psychology, 19, 323-339.

Carney, R.N., Levin, J.R. & Stackhouse, T.L. 1997. The Face-Name Mnemonic Strategy from a Different Perspective. Contemporary Educational Psychology, 22 (3), 399-412.

Guey, C-c., Cheng, Y-y. & Huang, L-j. 2003. Effect of keyword method on memory of word groups for Chinese learners of English. Paper presented at the Hawaii International Conference on Education, Jan 7-10, Honolulu.

Hall, J.W. & Fuson, K.C. 1988. The keyword method and presentation rates: Reply to Pressley (1987). Journal of Educational Psychology, 80(2), 251-252.

145

Hall, J.W. 1988. On the utility of the keyword mnemonic for vocabulary learning. Journal of Educational Psychology, 80(4), 554-562.

Hall, J.W. 1991. More on the utility of the keyword method. Journal of Educational Psychology, 83(1), 171-172.

Jitendra, A.K., Edwards, L.L., Sacks, G. & Jacobson, L.A. 2004. What research says about vocabulary instruction for students with learning disabilities. Exceptional Children, 70(3), 299-322.

Levin, M. & Levin, J. 1990. Scientific mnemonomies: Methods for maximizing more than memory. American Educational Research Journal, 27(2), 301-321.

McDaniel, M.A. & Pressley, M. 1989. Keyword and context instruction of new vocabulary meanings: Effects on text comprehension and memory. Journal of Educational Psychology, 81(2), 204-213.

Pressley, M. 1991. Comparing Hall (1988) with related research on elaborative mnemonics. Journal of Educational Psychology, 83(1), 165-170.

Pressley, M., Levin, J.R., Nakamura, G.V., Hope, D.J., Bispo, J.G. & Toye, A.R. 1980. The Keyword Method of Foreign Vocabulary Learning: An Investigation of Its Generalizability. Journal of Applied Psychology, 65(6), 635-642.

Rosenheck, M.B., Levin, M.E. & Levin, J.R. 1989. Learning botany concepts mnemonically: seeing the forest and the trees. Journal of Educational Psychology, 81, 196-203.

Thomas, M.H. & Wang, A.Y. 1996. Learning by the keyword mnemonic: Looking for long-term benefits. Journal of Experimental Psychology: Applied, 2(4), 330-342.

Uberti, H.Z., Scruggs, T.E. & Mastropieri, M.A. 2003. Keywords make the difference! Mnemonic instruction in inclusive classrooms. Teaching Exceptional Children, 35(3), 56-61.

Wang, A.Y., Thomas, M.H. & Ouellette, J.A.1992. Keyword mnemonic and retention of second-language vocabulary words. Journal of Educational Psychology, 84(4), 520-528.

Willoughby, T., Wood, E. & Khan, M. 1994. Isolating variables that impact on or detract from the effectiveness of elaboration strategies. Journal of Educational Psychology, 86, 279-289.

Yeung, S.S. & Heyworth, R.M. 1992. Teaching English Vocabulary to Cantonese-speaking Students with the Keyword Method. Education Journal, 20(2), 113-129.

Extensions to the keyword method

Numbered citations:

1. Levin, J.R., Shriberg, L.K., Miller, G.E., McCormack, C.B. & Levin, B.B. 1980. The keyword method in the classroom: How to remember the states and their capitals. The Elementary School Journal, 82, 185-91.

2. For example,
   McCormick, C.B. & Levin, J.R. 1984. A comparison of different prose-learning variations of the mnemonic keyword method. American Education Research

Journal, 21, 379-398.

Peters, E.E. & Levin, J.R. 1986. Effects of a mnemonic imagery strategy on good and poor readers' prose recall. Reading Research Quarterly, 21, 179-192.

Shriberg, L.K., Levin, J.R., McCormick, C.B. & Pressley, M. 1982. Learning about "famous" people via the mnemonic keyword method. Journal of Educational Psychology, 74, 238-247.

3. McCormick, C.B., Levin, J.R., Cykowski, F. & Danilovics, P. 1984. Mnemonic-strategy reduction of prose-learning interference. Educational Communication and Technology Journal, 32(3), 145-152.

4. McCormick, C.B. & Levin, J.R. 1984. A comparison of different prose-learning variations of the mnemonic keyword method. American Education Research Journal, 21, 379-398.

5. Rummel, N., Levin, J.R. & Woodward, M.M. 2003. Do pictorial mnemonic text-learning aids give students something worth writing about? Journal of Educational Psychology, 95(2), 327-334.

6. For example,
Carney, R.N. & Levin, J.R. 2000. Fading Mnemonic Memories: Here's Looking Anew, Again! Contemporary Educational Psychology, 25 (4), 499-508.
Carney, R.N. & Levin, J.R. 2000. Mnemonic instruction, with a focus on transfer. Journal of Educational Psychology, 92(4), 783-790.

7. Carney, R.N. & Levin, J.R. 2001. Remembering the Names of Unfamiliar Animals: Keywords as Keys to Their Kingdom. Applied Cognitive Psychology, 15, 133-143.

8. Carney, R.N. & Levin, J.R. 2003. Promoting higher-order learning benefits by building lower-order mnemonic connections. Applied Cognitive Psychology, 17, 563-575.

9. Morrison, C.R. & Levin, J.R. 1987. Degree of mnemonic support and students' acquisition of science facts. Educational Communication and Technology Journal, 35(2), 67-74.

Story method

Numbered citations:

1. Bower, G.H. & Clark, M.C. 1969. Narrative stories as mediators for serial learning. Psychonomic Science, 14, 181-182.

2. Bower, G.H. 1973. How to ... uh... remember. Psychology Today, 7, 63-69.

3. Bellezza, F.S. 1982. Updating memory using mnemonic devices. Cognitive Psychology, 14, 301-27.

4. Cornoldi, C. & De Beni, R. 1996. Mnemonics and metacognition. In Herrmann, D., McEvoy, C., Hertzog, C., Hertel, P. & Johnson, M.K. (eds). Basic and Applied Memory Research, Vol 2: Practical Applications, 237-253.

5. Hishitani, S. 1985. Coding strategies and imagery differences in memory. Japanese Psychological Research, 27, 154-162.

6. Boltwood, C.E. & Blick, K.A. 1970. The delineation and application of three mnemonic techniques. Psychonomic Science, 20, 339-341.

Other references:

Cook, N.M. 1989. The applicability of verbal mnemonics for different populations: a review. Applied Cognitive Psychology, 3, 3-22.

Delaney, P.F. & Knowles, M.E. 2005. Encoding Strategy Changes and Spacing Effects in the Free Recall of Unmixed Lists. Journal of Memory and Language, 52 (1), 120-130.

Drevenstedt, J. & Bellezza, F.S. 1993. Memory for self-generated narration in the elderly. Psychology and Aging, 8(2), 187-196.

Hill, R.D., Allen, C. & McWhorter, P. 1991. Stories as a mnemonic aid for older learners. Psychology and Aging, 6(3), 484-486.

Place method

Numbered citations:

1. DeBeni, R. & Cornoldi, C. 1985. Effects of the mnemotechnique of loci in the memorization of concrete words. Acta Psychologica, 60, 11-24.

2. Moè, A. & De Beni, R. 2004. Stressing the efficacy of the Loci method: oral presentation and the subject-generation of the Loci pathway with expository passages. Applied Cognitive Psychology, 19 (1), 95-106.

Other references:

Bellezza, F.S. 1983. The spatial-arrangement mnemonic. Journal of Educational Psychology, 75 (6), 830-837.

Gruneberg, M.M. 1992. The practical application of memory aids: Knowing how, knowing when, and knowing when not. In M.M. Gruneberg & P. Morris (eds), Aspects of memory, vol.1, London: Routledge, 2nd ed, pp 169-195.

De Beni, R., Moè, A. & Cornoldi, C. 1997. Learning from Texts or Lectures: Loci Mnemonics can Interfere with Reading but not with Listening. European Journal of Cognitive Psychology, 9 (4), 401–416.

Morris, P.E. 1979. Strategies for learning and recall. In M.M. Gruneberg & P.E. Morris (eds). Applied Problems in Memory. London: Academic Press.

Pegword Method

Numbered citations:

1. Morris, P.E. & Reid, R.L. 1970. Repeated use of mnemonic imagery. Psychonomic Science, 20, 337-338.

2. Carney, R.N. & Levin, J.R. 2010. Delayed mnemonic benefits for a combined pegword-keyword strategy, time after time, rhyme after rhyme. Applied Cognitive Psychology, In press.

3. Paivio, A. 1971. Imagery and verbal processes. New York: Holt, Rinehart and Winston.
   Santa, J.L., Ruskin, A.D. & Yio, A.J.H. 1973. Mnemonic systems in free recall. Psychological Reports, 32, 1163-70.

4. Delprato, D.J. & Baker, E.J. 1974. Concreteness of pegwords in two mnemonic systems. Journal of Experimental Psychology, 102, 520-522.

5. DiVesta, F.J. & Sunshine, P.M. 1974. The retrieval of abstract and concrete materials as functions of imagery, mediation and mnemonic aids. Memory and Cognition, 2, 340-344.

Link method

Numbered citations:

1. Bugelski, B.R. 1974. The image as mediator in one-trial paired-associate learning. III Sequential functions in serial lists. Journal of Experimental Psychology, 103, 298-303.
Delin, P.S. 1969. The learning to criterion of a serial list with and without mnemonic instructions. Psychonomic Science, 16, 169-170.

Coding mnemonic

Numbered citations:

1. Chase, W.G. & Ericsson, K.A. 1981. Skilled memory. In J.R. Anderson (ed.) Cognitive skills and their acquisition. Hillsdale, NJ: Erlbaum.

2. Higbee, K.L. 1997. Novices, Apprentices, and Mnemonists: Acquiring Expertise with the Phonetic Mnemonic. Applied Cognitive Psychology, 11, 147-161.

3. Patton, G.W.R. & Lantzy, P.D. 1987. Testing the limits of the phonetic mnemonic system. Applied Cognitive Psychology, 1, 263-71.
Patton, G.W.R., D'Agaro, W.R. & Gaudette, M.D. 1991.

The effect of subject-generated and experimenter-supplied code words on the phonetic mnemonic system. Applied Cognitive Psychology, 5, 135-48.

4. Kliegl, R., Smith, J., Heckhausen, J. & Baltes, P.B. 1987. Mnemonic Training for the Acquisition of Skilled Digit Memory. Cognition and Instruction, 4 (4), 203-223.

5. Bellezza, F.S., Six, L.S. & Phillips, D.S. 1992. A mnemonic for remembering long strings of digits. Bulletin of the Psychonomic Society, 30 (4), 271-274.

6. Hatano, G. & Kuhara, K. 1973. Production and use of mnemonic phrases in paired-associate learning with digits as response terms. Psychological Reports, 33, 923-930.

7. Higbee, K.L. 1988. You Memory: How it works and how to improve it. NY: Simon & Schuster, Inc.

Other references:

Morris, P.E. & Greer, P.J. 1984. The effectiveness of the phonetic mnemonic system. Human Learning, 3, 137-142.

Slak, S. 1970. Phonemic recoding of digital information. Journal of Experimental Psychology, 86, 398-406.

Slak, S. 1985. On phonetic and phonemic mnemonic systems: A reply to M.J. Dickel. Perceptual and Motor Skills, 61, 727-733.

Wilding, J. & Valentine, E. 1994. Mnemonic Wizardry with the Telephone Directory — But Stories are Another Story. British Journal of Psychology, 85, 501-509.

Mastering mnemonics

Numbered citations:

1. Baddeley, A.D. & Lieberman, K. 1980. Spatial working memory. In Nickerson, R.S. (ed.), Attention and Performance VIII: Hillsdale NJ: Erlbaum.
   Logie, R.H. 1986. Visuo-spatial processing in working memory. Quarterly Journal of Experimental Psychology, 38A, 229-47.

2. Brewer, W.F. 1980. Literary theory, rhetoric, and stylistics: Implications for psychology. In R. J. Shapiro, B. C. Bruce, & W. F. Brewer (Eds.), Theoretical issues in reading comprehension (pp. 221–239). Hillsdale, NJ: Erlbaum.

3. Bower, G.H. & Reitman, J.S. 1972. Mnemonic elaboration in multilist learning. Journal of Verbal Learning and Verbal Behavior, 11, 478-485.

4. Solso, R. L. 1995. Cognitive psychology (4th ed.). Boston: Allyn & Bacon.

5. Wilding, J. and Valentine, E. 1994. Memory champions. British Journal of Psychology, 85,231-244.

6. Cepeda, N.J. et al. 2008. Spacing Effects in Learning: A Temporal Ridgeline of Optimal Retention. Psychological Science, 19 (11), 1095-1102.

7. Taylor, K. & Rohrer, D. 2009. The effects of interleaved practice. Applied Cognitive Psychology, Published online 30 July.

8. Bjork, R. A. 1994. Memory and metamemory considerations in the training of human beings. In J.

Metcalfe, A. Shimamura, (Eds.), *Metacognition: Knowing about knowing* (pp. 185–205). Cambridge, MA: MIT Press.

Other references:

Higbee, K.L. 1988. You Memory: How it works and how to improve it. NY: Simon & Schuster, Inc.

Index

Printed in Great Britain
by Amazon